Reader's Digest
Wildlife Watch

Waterside & Coast in Autumn

Reader's Digest
Wildlife Watch

Waterside & Coast in Autumn

Published by
The Reader's Digest Association Limited
London • New York • Sydney • Montreal

Contents

Wildlife habitats and havens

Coast watch

Animals and plants in focus

Waterside watch

introduction

Illuminated by the sun as the mist clears on a September morning, an open, grassy hillside glows like a richly woven tapestry threaded with glinting gold. The bracken that covers the valley slopes has turned a golden russet and the dry grasses reflected in a clear stream flare bright yellow against the dark, peat-stained water, gleaming like a mirror beneath the arching, cobalt-blue sky.

A big, long-winged bird of prey, an osprey, appears cruising over the water, flashing white beneath chocolate brown, a dark mask over its eyes. Ospreys can often be seen over British waters at this time of year. They drop in, stay for a few days, then move on. They are among the more spectacular birds of passage – migrants that stop off to feed and rest on their way to their winter quarters in Africa. In autumn, a succession of these passing visitors arrive, all heading south. The sun may still have the golden glow of late summer, but autumn is closing in.

The magnificent osprey is a dedicated fish-catcher, with long, sharp claws and spiny pads beneath its toes for gripping slippery, struggling prey.

The extensive root systems of salt-resistant marram grass stabilise coastal sand dunes, and stop them being swept away by the winds and storms of autumn.

In early autumn, ponds are still teeming with small prey for the voracious great diving beetle. It hunts entirely underwater, carrying its air supply beneath its wing cases.

Home waters

For some of the fish that the osprey might catch, the season prompts a very different journey. Atlantic salmon, big and glossy from years spent feeding in the rich waters off Greenland, head for their home rivers in late summer and swim upstream to spawn. They favour the cool, shallow, oxygen-rich waters of the upper reaches, and to get there they are prepared to swim up rapids and leap over waterfalls. Some never make it, but drift exhausted into the shallows where they may fall prey to hungry otters, along with other salmon that have already spawned. An otter would not normally tackle such big fish, but a spent salmon makes a tempting prize.

While salmon are migrating upstream, the otters' favourite prey, eels, are going the other way (see pages 67–70). Salmon feed in the sea and spawn in rivers – eels do the opposite. They feed in freshwater for many years, but the time comes when, in early autumn, many get the urge to head downriver and out into the Atlantic Ocean to breed. They probably do not feed as they slip downstream, but the weight they have already gained to fuel their long journey makes them inviting prey.

Squabbling mallard

Fish are not the only animals with breeding in mind. While many birds are heading south to escape the winter, mallard ducks are beginning to pair up. They gather in large mixed-sex flocks on ponds and lakes, and the drakes, resplendent in their breeding plumage, compete to impress the females with the vigour of their displays. When a female approaches, the rivals may rear up in the water, whistling, but as she makes her choice the rejected males often turn on the victor and on each other, and the competitive display degenerates into a pecking, feather-pulling fight. The female is often forced to make her escape, chased by several males.

Mallard begin their breeding season unusually early. In autumn most waterfowl are more concerned with finding food and the productive waters of lowland lakes can attract huge flocks of diving ducks. Some of these, such as the tufted duck,

As insects become scarce in autumn, the bearded tits that live in reedbeds start to eat seeds, making high-pitched, 'pinging' calls as they flit from seed head to seed head.

When other pond plants have died back in late autumn, the water may still contain a splash of green *Riccia*, a floating, moss-like liverwort buoyed up by tiny air bubbles.

Otters hunt both on quiet, unpolluted rivers and on the rocky shores of the north and west. Seasonal fish migrations provide them with plenty of prey in autumn.

feed on small invertebrates including water fleas (see pages 77–78). Others, such as the pochard, eat mainly plant material. The shallow waters of Lough Neagh in Northern Ireland are rich in both types of food and regularly attract more than 20,000 pochard in autumn. They feed intensively throughout September and October, alongside tufted ducks, goldeneyes, coots and moorhens (see pages 56–61) and other waterbirds.

Many of the birds that feed on or near such lakes are winter visitors that have flown south from their summer breeding grounds in the far north. They include a variety of geese (see pages 62–66) and Bewick's swans that fly in from Arctic Siberia. The swans begin to arrive in October and by late autumn there may be 2000 or more on the East Anglian Ouse Washes, accompanied by perhaps 200 whooper swans from Iceland. Wilder and more goose-like than the familiar mute swan, with distinctive black and yellow bills, these tundra swans are among the most spectacular sights of autumn wetlands.

Gleaming mudflats

Farther downstream, the salt marshes flanking the tidal reaches of rivers may still retain a blue haze of flowering sea lavender, while nearer the water the glasswort growing on the mudflats turns bright red with the advancing season. These salt-marsh plants (see pages 121–125) are specially adapted to survive submersion by salty seawater, and many rely on the ebb and flow of the tide to spread the seeds that they produce in late summer and autumn.

These seeds are devoured eagerly by small birds, including greenfinches, yellowhammers, linnets and meadow pipits, which swarm over land that is exposed at low water. Meanwhile large flocks of lapwings gather on nearby silt lagoons to feast on small animals swept in by the tide. Out near the tide line a variety of longer billed waders, such as curlews, godwits and redshanks, probe the mudflats for worms and molluscs (see pages 24–27). As the tide comes in it pushes the waders up the shore until they are forced together in dense roosts in the salt marsh, waiting for the tide to ebb again.

Many of these waders return to the same remote marshes each autumn because these places offer security at a time when the birds are especially vulnerable. Autumn is the time of the annual moult when many birds lose so many feathers that they cannot fly properly, if at all. The mudflats of Snettisham on The Wash, for example, provide a secure moulting roost for more than 70,000 waders including bar-tailed godwits, grey plovers, redshanks, sanderlings, knots and dunlins (see pages 94–99).

Sandy beaches deserted by the summer crowds attract parties of sanderlings. These waders scurry along the tide line on blurred legs, probing for submerged prey.

Driftwood swept ashore by autumn gales may carry clusters of stalked goose barnacles, which normally live in the open sea attached to floating debris.

The rusty red head of the male pochard makes him easy to identify among the huge flocks of diving ducks that gather on lakes, but the dull grey and brown females are far less conspicuous.

Seasonal storms

Many birds, including oystercatchers, roost on coastal shingle banks such as those that form the vast, wild headland of Dungeness (see pages 36–41). These banks are bleak, barren places at the best of times but when they are lashed by the seasonal storms of autumn they are among the most exposed of all coastal habitats. They can be reshaped overnight by the pounding waves, uprooting any plants that may have managed to get a grip on the shingle over summer.

The storms of autumn leave the shore littered with seaweed, driftwood and dead animals, including fish, crabs, sea urchins, starfish and seabirds. Occasionally, more exotic objects are swept up, such as violet sea snails and the highly venomous Portuguese man-of-war jellyfish. The waves push all this decaying flotsam into a long, straggling heap known as the strand line, where it becomes home to countless small animals such as kelp flies and sand hoppers (see pages 114–115). The mixture of live animals and edible debris attracts birds, including turnstones, ringed plovers, rock pipits and even skylarks, as well as scavenging crows, greater black-backed gulls and foxes.

Atlantic storms may also sweep living birds far off their autumn migration routes, carrying American species such as the greater yellowlegs across the ocean to the Scilly Isles and other western shores. These autumn vagrants are usually doomed to spend the rest of their often short lives far from their original homes, since they have no way of making the return journey.

Despite such storms, one coastal species chooses this time of year to breed. On rocky western shores, female grey seals haul themselves ashore ready to give birth after a long gestation of nearly a year (see pages 86–89). They are soon followed by the big bull grey seals, fiercely claiming territories, which they then guard aggressively. When the pups are born the females mate again almost straight away, but they stay onshore for three weeks until the pups are old enough to be left alone for a few hours. By the time the pups are ready to go to sea, some five weeks later, the mists of autumn have given way to the numbing chill of winter.

The great humpback whales that are occasionally sighted off British coasts in autumn are probably seasonal migrants, heading south to spend the winter in the tropics.

Gutweed, or *Enteromorpha* seaweed, is a vital food for the thousands of brent geese that arrive from their Arctic breeding grounds to spend the winter on coastal mudflats.

The speckled skin of a young plaice lying on a bed of gravel helps to conceal it from hungry bass and cod that swim inshore to feed just below the tide line.

Wildlife habitats and havens

- Reedbeds – wetland wildernesses
- Wildlife along the towpath
- Life in tidal mudflats
- Coastal harbours
- Rocky shores
- The shingle outpost of Dungeness

Reedbeds – wetland wildernesses

The rustling reedbeds that cover large areas of wetland make ideal refuges for wildlife. In among the tall reeds, thousands of small birds gather to roost in the twilight, filling the air with their song.

A large reedbed is one of the few habitats that is virtually impenetrable to humans. Tall reeds, with their plumed seed heads, sprout from shallow water or wet mud, and grow so densely that exploring beyond the margins of an extensive reedbed is almost impossible, whether on foot or by boat. This makes reedbeds places where wild animals can live undisturbed by people.

Specialised wetland animals that are scarce elsewhere, such as the fast-declining water vole and the highly threatened bittern, make their homes there, but reedbeds also attract visitors from drier habitats. Many birds use them as secure roosts for the night, especially in autumn. Yet the security that is so valuable to wildlife can make reedbeds frustrating places for people to visit, because clear sightings of animals are often tantalisingly difficult to obtain.

Although reedbeds are very productive habitats, the plant life usually consists of just a few fast-growing species.

The dominant plant is the common reed, a tall grass that grows to a height of 3m (10ft) or more. It spreads across the wetlands by means of rhizomes (creeping, underground stems) which sprout from the shallows to form a continuous thicket of densely packed stalks. Initially green, the reeds turn straw yellow as late summer turns to autumn and their dark, greyish purple flower heads turn into feathery, silver-brown sprays of seeds.

Tall plants

Other tall marshland plants form dense beds of their own. They include reed sweet-grass, canary-grass and various sedges and rushes. The sturdy bulrush, sometimes known as reedmace, is just as vigorous as common reed and makes an imposing waterside feature in autumn with its large, brown, club-like seed heads.

Yellow flag iris can cover corners of lakes and ponds with small reed-like thickets. By autumn its bright yellow flowers are long gone, but the seed capsules remain on the

flower stems, swollen to large pods packed with big brown seeds. Other marshland flowers may still be in bloom in the more open areas between stands of tall reeds.

▲ A pair of bearded tits may raise two or three broods of young during a breeding season that lasts well into early autumn. These birds are seldom seen away from large reedbeds.

Greater spearwort often bears its yellow buttercup-like flowers into early autumn and hemp-agrimony may still be in bloom, its mops of nectar-rich pinkish purple flowers acting like magnets to late-flying butterflies, such as the comma and small tortoiseshell.

Invading scrub

Like some other types of grass, common reed is vigorous and eventually spreads over large areas, often to the exclusion of other vegetation. A deep layer of dead leaves and stems accumulates on top of the mat of rhizomes at the base of the reeds, decaying very slowly and inhibiting the growth of other plants.

This dense tangle of rhizomes and reed litter has been found to act as a water filter, removing organic pollutants that enter the water from farmland or even from sewage outfalls. The discovery has inspired the creation of many new reedbeds in wetlands where such pollution is a problem, to the benefit of the wetland wildlife.

As reed litter builds up, it eventually rises above the water level and starts to dry out. Willow and alder scrub may then invade the reedbed from the fringes, creating islands of tangled wet woodland that make ideal breeding sites for small birds.

▼ Reedbeds gradually expand and encroach on lakes, eventually eliminating the open water. Willow and alder woodland then begins to replace the reeds around the margins of the bed, and in time both the lake and reedbed disappear.

AUTUMN ROOSTS

In autumn, huge gatherings of birds arrive at dusk to roost in reedbeds. Groups of starlings gather together to form immense flocks that swirl through the sky like smoke before settling to huddle in the sanctuary afforded by the densely packed reed stems. As they land, the birds twitter and jostle for space, ideally near the centre of the reedbed where they are safer from predators. As dawn approaches, the twittering reaches a crescendo. Then there is a sudden hush and

House martins are gregarious but they rarely mix with swallows or sand martins when roosting in the reedbeds in autumn. At this time, their white underparts are tinged buff.

▲ From September starling numbers are swollen by continental migrants, attracted by the milder climate.

part of the flock bursts up into the sky to leave the roost. This may happen several times until all the starlings have left the reedbed for their daytime feeding grounds.

Thousands of sand martins, swallows, house martins and yellow wagtails congregate in some reedbeds before embarking on their annual migration to Africa. During the late 1960s a reedbed roost on the Ouse Washes in eastern England harboured an estimated 2 million sand martins. Such vast roosts are now unknown, largely because the birds themselves are less common.

The birds build up their reserves of energy by feeding on the swarming reed aphids and clouds of midges each evening before retreating to the reeds for the night. As they feed, they are targeted by aerial predators such as the sparrowhawk and the hobby – a long-winged falcon related to the peregrine and kestrel. Unlike them, the hobby is itself a long-distance migrant. It spends the winter in Africa, but delays its departure to exploit this concentration of potential prey. A high-speed hunter, the hobby is fast enough to catch a swift on the wing, but despite its deadly speed and power, the swallows and martins often try to defend themselves by flying up and diving at the raptor in an attempt to drive it away.

Usually seen only in brief glimpses before it dives into cover, Cetti's warbler favours scrubby reedbed margins. It is the only warbler that remains in the vicinity of reedbeds all year.

Eventually the reedbed will be completely taken over by scrub unless the site is artificially managed to prevent this happening.

Late dragonflies
A succession of dragonflies cruise the reedbed waterways during the summer, and some are still active in autumn. They include the powerful common hawker, southern hawker and migrant hawker, which patrol the open water endlessly in search of small flying insects to snatch and eat.

Darters have a different technique, perching on stems and darting up like flycatchers to seize passing victims. The ruddy darter is often on the wing until late October. The yellow-ochre females are inconspicuous but the males are a rich blood-red. The more abundant common darter is slightly larger and the paler red males and amber females can be distinguished from ruddy darters by their yellow-striped legs.

Common and ruddy darters can often be seen laying their eggs in the open areas between reedbeds well into autumn. The males and females fly in tandem as the females dip their tails in the water to release their

eggs. These lie dormant over winter. The larvae then hatch in spring and develop underwater among the roots of reedbed plants such as bulrushes, emerging as winged adults in late summer.

Tits and warblers
The reed litter at the base of the reedbed is the nesting habitat of the bearded tit, a reedbed specialist that remains throughout the year and may still be feeding young in mid-September. The gentle pinging calls of bearded tits may be heard echoing above the rustling of reeds disturbed by the autumn breeze. The calls intensify as the birds flit over the reedbeds, their rich tawny plumage blending in with the straw-coloured reeds. Occasionally – but only for a moment – a male may perch at the top of a reed stem in full view, allowing a glimpse of his 'moustache' marking, apparently drooping from a tiny golden beak. However, despite its name, the bearded tit has no 'beard'.

▲ A migrant hawker dragonfly patrols the reeds. Small squadrons of them cruise along open channels, snapping up flies and midges well into November, until overnight frosts kill off the last surviving dragonflies.

▶ The crimson body of the male ruddy darter makes it an eyecatching sight as it perches on a stem watching for prey.

ACCIDENTAL CONSERVATION

In some reedbeds, reeds are cut for thatching, a trade that is experiencing a revival as historic buildings are restored. However, reed cutting can threaten some animals, particularly wetland moths, the caterpillars of which live and feed inside hollow reed stems. Reedbed conservation to protect the more glamorous swallowtail butterfly – a species that, in Britain, is restricted to wetlands – has also helped to conserve rare moths, including the reed leopard and Fenn's wainscot, which might otherwise die out.

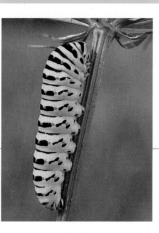

Despite its gaudy appearance, the swallowtail butterfly's caterpillar is well camouflaged.

A male reed bunting still in his summer breeding plumage is a striking bird, the white collar 'moustache' making a bold contrast with his jet black head.

Several species of warbler nest in and around reedbeds, but most migrate to the tropics at the end of summer. Warblers – and other birds – on migration from farther north often stop off to feed in southern reedbeds on their way south in autumn.

Sedge warblers are among the last to leave and gather in great numbers in south coast reedbeds, such as Radipole in Weymouth, Dorset. They consume vast numbers of the plum-reed aphids that plague the reeds, often almost doubling their body weight in preparation for the arduous non-stop flight to sub-Saharan Africa.

Another late migrant that often feeds in reedbeds before leaving for the tropics is the grasshopper warbler, a species best known for its strange mechanical, reeling song. A few aquatic warblers, a species that is threatened globally, turn up in southern reedbeds each autumn on the way to Africa from their continental nesting grounds.

Noisy residents

One species of warbler stays in and around southern and eastern reedbeds throughout the autumn and winter. Cetti's warbler, which was first recorded in Britain in 1961, is a colonist from the Mediterranean region. It favours willow thickets within or beside the reedbeds, and has such skulking habits that it is difficult to see, although its explosive bursts of song are extremely distinctive. Since it does not migrate like other wetland warblers, its numbers may suffer in years when autumn gives way to a hard winter.

Some reedbed birds, such as the reed bunting, are more conspicuous. This common resident may be feeding a third brood of young by September and, before it moults into its drabber winter plumage, the black-headed male makes a handsome sight as he perches upright on a tall reed stem, flicking his tail and 'chinging' persistently. Reed buntings may stay on and around reedbeds throughout the autumn and winter.

One of the best ways to look for the more elusive reedbed birds is to watch from a hide on a wetland nature reserve. A patient scan of the water's edge, where fringing reeds rise out of the shallows, may be rewarded by a glimpse of a water rail. Although notorious for its secrecy, this slender relative of the more common moorhen can sometimes be seen creeping along the fringes of the reeds, its barred

In lakes where the water is rich in nutrients, the margins often become fringed with reeds, bulrushes and other waterside plants. After a few years, whole bays can become choked with the plants and a reedbed is created.

The water rail's narrow body enables it to slip easily through the reed stems as it hunts for prey, which it seizes in its strong red dagger of a bill.

flanks helping it to blend with the stems. It may betray its presence with startling squeals that sound more like a pig than a bird.

Reedbeds also harbour the most elusive of all wetland birds – the bittern. This large, striped brown heron is one of the rarest British birds. Fewer than 30 pairs breed in Britain, mainly in the reedbeds of Leighton Moss in Lancashire and Minsmere in Suffolk, but in autumn some disperse more widely and are joined by migrants from the Continent. They are still very scarce, however, and their cryptic plumage makes them very difficult to see. If a bittern senses danger, it points its bill skywards to mimic the reed stems, and may even sway slowly to match the motion of the wind-blown reeds.

Basking grass snakes

Piles of old reed and sedge – perhaps the remains of a swan's nest – may provide basking places for grass snakes. These semi-aquatic reptiles favour marshes and swamps, where they hunt for frogs, newts and even fish.

Earlier in the year, in June or July, the females lay their batches of creamy, leather-shelled eggs within moist, rotting heaps of reed litter. The warmth generated by the process of decay makes

the heaps ideal natural incubators, and from late August to mid-September the hatchling snakes struggle from their shells and burrow out into the marshy world of the reedbed.

Pencil-sized versions of their parents, the baby snakes must fend for themselves from the start. They wriggle their way through the reed litter, searching for appropriately small prey, such as tiny froglets and insects, although they are equally at risk of falling victim to predators such as herons. Those that survive are forced to find winter refuges as the temperature drops and by November both adults and young will have slipped into the deep sleep of hibernation.

Vanishing voles

A distinctive 'plop' from a narrow water channel passing through a reedbed may be caused by a water vole diving in to evade danger. Once commonly found on wetlands and rivers, this portly rodent is in serious trouble over much of Britain due to a combination of factors. In many areas it has suffered from the destruction of the extensive wetlands that once flanked many lowland rivers, limiting its options and making it an easier target for mink, the predator that is usually blamed for the water vole's decline.

This American species was originally bred in captivity for its valuable fur, but escaped

The bulrush, one of the most instantly recognisable of reedbed plants, is widespread in much of lowland England and grows to a height of 2m (6ft 6in) or more. Its relative, the lesser bulrush, is patchy in distribution and is most often found in the East Anglian fens and the south-east. Both species favour shallow, marginal waters.

▲ The seed heads of bulrushes eventually ripen, rupture and burst, releasing masses of tiny seeds. However, the bulrush – like the common reed – spreads mainly by rhizomes (creeping, root-like underground stems). In the past, the fluffy seed heads were used to stuff mattresses.

The grass snake is an excellent swimmer and spends much of its time hunting frogs and fish among the marshy margins of extensive reedbeds.

into the wild and established breeding populations in many wetlands, including reedbeds. The mink is an expert swimmer, but it spends a lot of its time out of the water. It is bolder than most native mammals, and it can sometimes be watched for some minutes as it grooms its fur on a mat of reeds.

The mink is often mistaken for the otter – a much bigger, more elusive wetland hunter. A powerful swimmer, the otter penetrates deep into the heart of the reedbed where it chases eels and other fish. Otters are becoming more numerous as water quality improves, and many reedbeds now support

A water vole can thrive in the sanctuary of reedbeds, moving easily through the vertical stems. These rodents often emerge on to exposed areas of mud at the foot of the reeds to eat their plant food at leisure.

small populations of a few breeding pairs. Some nature wardens are building artificial otter dens at wetland nature reserves to encourage them to take up residence.

Autumn seed
The smallest mammal to frequent reedbeds is the diminutive harvest mouse. In late summer it slings its tennis-ball-sized nests between the reed stems, weaving shredded

leaf blades into a nursery for its young. From autumn onwards, the plentiful seed from the seed heads at the top of the reed stems provides a rich harvest of food for these mice, as well as the many small seed-eating birds that forage through the reedbeds from autumn into the bleaker months of winter.

Mice, voles and other small animals may attract hungry foxes into reedbeds. Roe deer sometimes venture into the

drier parts, where they can lie up with little risk of being disturbed. Even close to human habitation, reedbeds can provide guaranteed security for wild animals that is becoming increasingly rare in the modern world.

The flowering heads of the common reed mature during autumn, when the seeds are shed into the wind or on to the fur and feathers of visiting animals and birds.

Wildlife along the towpath

Once part of a busy transport network, many canals are now tranquil havens for wetland wildlife. In autumn, the water glows with rich, reflected colours while fruits and late-blooming flowers sustain insects and birds.

Standing beside a leafy, disused canal on a warm day in early autumn, listening to the breeze in the willows and the occasional throaty alarm call of a moorhen, it may be hard to imagine it as a legacy from heavy industry. In such a place of utter tranquillity, the still or gently flowing water is dotted with floating leaves and the occasional spreading ripple set up by an insect or feeding fish.

Even where canals pass through the hearts of great cities, they are often peaceful refuges, remote from the bustle and noise of the streets.

Yet it was not always so, for in the 18th and early 19th centuries the canals were vital arteries of commerce, the equivalent of later railways and motorways – and in some ways more efficient than either. A barge hauled by a single horse was able to transport up to

▲ **For most of its 35-mile length, the Monmouthshire and Brecon Canal is a rural waterway. It flows through the beautiful Brecon Beacons.**

▶ **A water vole will eat reeds and grasses that grow at the canal sides, discarding the tougher parts of the plants and leaving them scattered about the feeding area.**

30 tonnes of cargo at a time – a marvellous feat when the alternative was to use strings of packhorses or to haul carts by roads that for much of the time were bogged down in mud. Canal barges were reliable, and they plied the canals in such numbers they were able to deliver the raw materials and products of industry in a steady flow, rather like a vast pipeline.

Decay and revival

Two of the earliest canals in Britain were the Sankey Navigation – now known as the St Helen's Canal – and the Bridgewater Canal, which opened in 1761. The heyday of canal building lasted for another 80 years or so, and by the 1830s over 6400km (4000 miles) of canals threaded the British landscape. Within a few decades, however, the canals began to be eclipsed by a new form of transport – the railway. During the early 20th century the railways gradually leached away the trade that sustained the canal companies, and by the mid 1940s the canal network was in serious decline. Much of it was abandoned, and some of the canals built over higher ground became dry ditches as the water drained away.

Others survived, however, and many have been restored to working order. Despite this, the volume of traffic is so low that even working canals are now valuable refuges for wild plants and animals. Many have been awarded conservation status and more than 80 Sites of Special Scientific Interest

The overgrown margins of silted-up canals can make a suitable habitat for two of Britain's most secretive birds – the water rail and the little grebe. The skulking habits and plumage of the water rail, a red-billed relative of the moorhen and coot, make it very hard to see, but it can often be detected by its pig-like squeal.

A small brown bird swimming on the water is likely to be a little grebe. It will dive beneath the surface if disturbed and often swims some way before reappearing, checking the coast is clear and slipping into the marginal vegetation.

▶ The shy water rail haunts the dense vegetation fringing some of the more overgrown canals, emerging to hunt the small snails, insects, fish and other creatures that inhabit the shallows.

◀ Canals are ideal habitats for little grebes, which prefer still or slow-flowing water. They are more often heard than seen, giving loud 'whinnying' calls.

(SSSIs) are associated with canals in England alone. Roughly half of these have been designated because of their aquatic plants, but others are important sites for birds and other animals.

Shady margins

Canal banks are often shaded by the foliage of willow and alder trees. Both are broad-leaved deciduous trees that thrive in the wet conditions of the canalside, and even survive with their roots in waterlogged soil. Alder can be identified in autumn by its distinctive seed-bearing fruits, which resemble

the cones of a conifer tree. They are green in summer, but as they ripen they turn dark brown, remaining on the tree throughout the winter.

Even in autumn, plants may be in bloom along the towpath, attracting a variety of insects. The sky-blue flowers of water forget-me-not, for example, can be seen nestling among the lush grass of canal banks as late as October.

Indian balsam – a spectacular introduction from southern Asia – may also be in bloom, although many of the flowers will have set seeds in pods that explode when touched.

Other common bankside plants such as purple loosestrife will have set seed, too. During the summer purple loosestrife's mauve flowers, along with those of teasel and thistle, are an

◀ Pioneering plants colonise small cracks and ledges on the walls of locks and sluices. Their decaying remains accumulate in the crevices, allowing more plants to take root.

▲ Water forget-me-not can grow in anything up to 50cm (20in) of water. Its dainty yellow-eyed flowers appear in profusion along many canals between June and October.

important source of nectar for the brimstone butterfly, a striking yellow (male) or greenish (female) species that can often be seen on the wing in autumn.

Canal plants

The still waters of a canal provide excellent growing conditions for aquatic plants. Some lurk out of sight in the murky depths, but others lie on the water surface or grow up to form lush thickets of marginal vegetation.

Along the canal edge, or where disused canals have silted up, plants that are rooted in submerged soil and flower above the water's surface – known as emergent plants – take precedence. They include the arrowhead, aptly named for the shape of its leaves, which rise vertically from the water. In summer it has delicate, white, three-petalled flowers, arranged in whorls around a spike to attract passing aquatic insects, but by September the flowers are replaced by globular fruits.

Branched bur-reed is a widespread plant of shallow canal margins. It has rather nondescript iris-like leaves but the female flowers form

▶ Male and female catkins of common alder grow on the same tree and the cone-like fruits ripen in autumn.

◀ The arrowhead is a perennial plant that prefers shallow, unpolluted water. It grows on clay soil.

ornate star-like burrs that are carried on leafy, branched spikes. In autumn the flowers develop two-seeded fruits. A related plant, the unbranched bur-reed, carries its flowers and fruits on a single spike that lies near the surface of shallow canal waters.

Many rushes and sedges grow along canal banks. They can be distinguished by the profile of their stems – those of rushes are round, but the stems of sedges are triangular.

One of the most impressive is the great marsh sedge, which can grow to 1.5m (5ft) tall and is common on canal banks throughout Britain. The flowering rush, actually a relative of the arrowhead, is in bloom from July to September, bearing clusters of bright pink three-petalled flowers that develop into purple egg-shaped fruits later in the year.

Water starwort is another common canal plant. There are seven species and each has

two types of leaf that can be mistaken for those of two completely different plants. The underwater leaves are blade-like, while those on the surface form a floating rosette. The rosette supports tiny yellow flowers that become tiny green nutlets in autumn.

Green carpets

Not all the plants floating on the water are anchored to the canal bottom. Some are completely free-living – in the still waters that they favour there is no danger of being swept away by currents. One of the most attractive is frogbit, which resembles a miniature, white-flowered water-lily, with

CANAL-LOVING BATS

To a bat, a disused canal tunnel is like an artificial cave, ideal for roosting during the day and hibernating in winter. The Greywell tunnel on the Basingstoke Canal is the largest roost site for bats in Britain, harbouring more than 12,000 bats of several species. The partly caved-in tunnel is impassable and plans to restore it were abandoned because of the bats.

Two species particularly associated with canal tunnels are Natterer's and Daubenton's bats.

The tunnel between Fleckley and Saddinton on the Grand Union Canal in Leicestershire is especially good for these two species. Both are active in early autumn, which is their main mating season, and as dusk falls they can often be seen hunting over the still waters of the canal for caddis flies and other insects.

Daubenton's bat is usually found near water and is the species most often seen flying low over a canal as dusk fades to night.

tiny 'lily pads' for leaves. Water-lilies, however, are not free-floating. The frogbit's leaves are linked by long runners. Its flowers develop into oval dark green fruits in autumn, and release seeds that sink to the bottom of the canal. There they grow into young plants that rise to the surface the following spring, along with others that develop from dormant winter buds that sink in the same way.

Similar to frogbit in their floating habit, but much smaller, the duckweeds frequently form extensive green carpets over the still or slow-moving waters of canals. Water birds have little trouble manoeuvring through this layer of greenery, since the individual plants are very small, with tiny leaves. However, duckweed can block

out light that would otherwise reach the water below and this impedes the growth of submerged water plants.

The stoneworts, of which there are 30 species native to Britain, look like flowering plants, but are actually an advanced group of algae. Their name refers to a brittle, crunchy coating of calcium carbonate (lime) that the plants secrete. This is a by-product of the way the algae use dissolved bicarbonate in the water as a source of carbon for the photosynthesis of sugar. By contrast, most plants and algae use carbon dioxide gas from the air.

Diving insects
The still waters of some canals can suffer from pollution, but even the most polluted canals usually support some form of

◄ In autumn the banks of this canal in Macclesfield glow with the rich red of fruiting hawthorn as the marginal water plants start to die back for the winter.

▲ Canalside vegetation makes a rich hunting ground for birds such as this young grey heron, which is still in its relatively drab juvenile plumage.

animal life. Among the most remarkable survivors are hoverfly larvae, better known as rat-tailed maggots. Their name is apt, for each larva has a soft, legless body and a long, extendible tail. This distinctive feature is the key to the maggot's success. Polluted water often contains very little oxygen, all concentrated near the surface. The maggot's tail acts as a telescopic breathing tube that extends up to this oxygen-bearing layer, enabling it to draw oxygen into its gills.

Cleaner water contains a much greater variety of animals, including the great diving beetle, which can grow to an impressive 45mm (1⅜in) long. It uses its hair-fringed hind legs to propel itself in pursuit of prey, such as tadpoles and even small fish. The beetle carries an air supply in a bubble trapped by its wing cases, and replenishes it at the surface at intervals.

Jet-propelled larvae

Many of the animals that live in the depths of canals are the larvae of flying insects such as caddis flies, dragonflies and damselflies. The adult phases of such creatures are often short-lived, with just a few weeks or even days on the wing before they mate, lay eggs and die. The larval stage of their life is protracted by comparison, lasting up to five

CANAL FISH

A number of freshwater fish live in canals. Roach are common largely because of their broad diet. They will feed on a variety of insect larvae, crustaceans and molluscs, but can also survive on rotting plantlife, algae and plankton.

The deep-bodied, bronze-coloured common bream is especially well suited to the silty bottoms of canals where it feeds on midge larvae and worms, which it sucks up along with the silty sediment. It uses its sensitive taste buds to sort out the food from the silt, squirting the unwanted material out through its gills.

Another fish well able to live in canals is the tench, a greenish fish with a distinctive squared tail. It feeds on molluscs and insect larvae and is unusually tolerant of the low oxygen levels and high temperatures that are typical of city canals. In late autumn tench like to bury themselves in mud for the winter and the clay that was originally used to line canals is ideal for this purpose.

▲ Overgrown, murky canal waters, often dappled by the shade of overhanging branches, create ideal hunting conditions for pike. The deep cover enables them to launch surprise attacks on smaller fish.

► The warm, slow-flowing, often cloudy waters of canals are frequently low in oxygen. Common bream are well able to tolerate this and are often abundant.

years in some species, and they are active throughout the autumn and beyond.

Known as nymphs, the drab-coloured larvae of damselflies and dragonflies are fearsome predators that eat other aquatic insects and small fish, seizing them in highly adapted jaws that can be suddenly extended like mechanical grabs. A damselfly nymph can be recognised by its three paddle-like tails, which are in fact gills. A dragonfly nymph has a set of gills housed in its anal cavity, which is adapted to draw in water and pump it out again.

The grass snake is quite at home swimming in the still water of a canal with or without a floating carpet of duckweed.

This doubles as a jet propulsion mechanism when the nymph needs to escape an enemy such as a large fish.

Amber wings

An adult dragonfly is as spectacular as its nymph is drab. One of the species most likely to be seen in autumn is the brown hawker, a large, dark brown dragonfly with yellow markings on the female, and blue and yellow on the male. The hawker's most distinctive feature is its wings, which have a wonderful amber glow. It can be seen well into October, flying tirelessly back and forth over canals in search of airborne insect prey.

Canals also harbour larger hunters such as the grass snake. This excellent swimmer

▲ An all-year-round resident, the kingfisher is a shy bird but its colourful plumage may be more conspicuous in autumn.

► After years of decline, otters are making a comeback to freshwater systems throughout Britain. The improved water conditions in many canals have probably helped.

favours still waters, so canals are ideal and probably important to the creature's survival in Britain. As it slips through the water, the grass snake holds its head up, on the alert for small amphibians and other animals to catch and swallow whole.

Silted-up canals make excellent hunting grounds for the grey heron, which wades stealthily through the shallow margins looking for fish and frogs. Every now and then it

freezes, transfixed by the sight of possible prey below the surface. Then it strikes, extending its long neck with great speed to spear its victim with its dagger-like bill.

In autumn, faster-moving water near locks and weirs may attract the grey wagtail, an active little grey and yellow bird that flutters along the water's edge, catching insects from just above the surface.

Grey wagtails breed mainly near upland streams and rivers in the summer, but in some regions they nest on ledges beneath canal bridges.

Cleaner canals may even attract otters, which cannot tolerate the water pollution that once affected many waterways. Once in steep decline, otters are now on the increase and have even set up territories on urban canals.

By contrast the water vole is on the retreat in many parts of Britain, owing to habitat loss and predation by feral mink. The vole still flourishes on several unpolluted canals, however, provided they have plenty of plant cover near the water's edge. It is possible that the sensitive restoration of canalside habitats may play a vital part in saving the water vole from extinction.

A female mallard keeps a watchful eye out for danger while her brood of ducklings tests the water. Broods as young as this can be seen on canals as late as October.

WILDLIFE WATCH

Where can I see canal wildlife?

1 The Caledonian Canal passes through several lochs amid the spectacular scenery of the Scottish Highlands, offering the chance to see hunting ospreys and eagles.

2 The Montgomery Canal in mid-Wales is managed for wildlife by British Waterways, and is noted for its rare aquatic plants. For more information, visit www.montgomerycanal.co.uk

3 The Prees Branch of the Shropshire Union Canal is managed as a nature reserve by the Shropshire Wildlife Trust. Telephone 01743 284280 or visit www.shropshire wildlifetrust.org.uk

4 Cromforde Canal Nature Reserve is managed by Derbyshire Wildlife Trust and is one of the top sites for birds in the county. Telephone 01636 677711.

5 The Basingstoke Canal in Surrey and Hampshire, run by the Basingstoke Canal Authority, is regarded as one of the best canals for wildlife. Telephone 01252 370073.

6 Camley Street Natural Park on London's Regent's Canal is run by the London Wildlife Trust. Telephone 020 7254 7186, or visit www.wildlifetrust.org.uk/london

● For information on canals across the country, contact British Waterways. Telephone 01923 201120 or visit www.british-waterways.org

Life in tidal mudflats

The unstable mudflats that flank tidal river estuaries are hostile habitats for most marine life. Yet some animals are able to survive in the mud, flourishing in numbers large enough to attract flocks of hungry birds.

Estuaries can seem bleak, lifeless places, especially on a grey autumn day at low tide, when the river dwindles to a narrow channel flowing between drab-looking expanses of treacherous mud. The lower levels of these tidal mudflats are quite bare of vegetation, and just beneath the surface the mud is devoid of oxygen, making it stagnant and foul-smelling. The temperature of the mud can fluctuate wildly when it is exposed to the air and, when the rising tide covers it, the water salinity changes constantly as fresh river water is pushed upstream by the incoming flood.

Only a few specialised types of marine invertebrates are able to tolerate such a hostile combination of factors, but those few enjoy an almost limitless supply of food in the form of plant and animal remains buried in the mud, or lying on its surface. This enables such invertebrates to multiply prolifically but, since they spend their entire lives hidden in the mud, often the only signs of their presence are the wading birds that flock to feed upon them.

The mud is formed from fine particles of silt suspended in moving water. Both the river flowing off the land and the incoming tide contain silt. Where the river meets the flood tide its flow stops, and the silt particles sink through the slack water to settle on the bottom. The salt in the tidal water also makes the tiny particles clump together, so they are heavier and more likely to settle, and they build up as level mudflats, which are exposed as the tide ebbs away.

◀ Some waders such as this bar-tailed godwit have very long bills, enabling them to probe deeply into the mud for lugworms and other buried prey.

▶ Glasswort is one of the most important colonising plants of higher-level mudflats. It is able to tolerate both immersion in sea water and exposure to air.

▼ As the receding tide in the Severn Estuary carves ripples in the mud, burrowing animals retreat to safety before they are snatched by hungry birds.

COCKLES AND COCKLE EATERS

Thousands of empty *Hydrobia* shells may accumulate among the strand line debris cast up by the tide. The living animals occur in vast densities on the mudflats of the lower shore.

More material is dropped with every tide, constantly building on the existing layers.

The main channel of the estuary is kept free of mud by the scouring action of the ebb tide as it pours out to sea twice a day. The flowing water cuts deep channels through the mud and at low water their depth reveals the thickness of the silt deposit.

Deep in the mud

Digging into a mudflat reveals distinct layers. The mud just beneath the smooth surface tends to be light coloured and pleasant smelling, but farther down it is much darker and has the sulphurous smell of rotten eggs. This is produced by anaerobic bacteria as they break down the organic matter that is deposited along with the silt. Anaerobic

Cockles often occur at high densities on mudflats, although since they live just below the surface they are not usually visible.

Like most bivalve (two-shelled) molluscs, a cockle has a pair of siphons that protrude from between its open shells. One siphon takes in sea water containing food and oxygen, and the water is then expelled through the other siphon. Cockles have very short siphons, so they burrow only a short way into the sand or mud. This makes them more vulnerable to predators than species that burrow deeper.

Their defence is to have thick shells that clamp tightly together. Few birds can open them, but oystercatchers can prise them apart or hammer a hole in their shells with their long, powerful bills. Some gulls have learned a more dramatic method. Holding a large cockle, the gull flies over an area of hard ground and drops the shell from a great height, swooping down to reach the ground before another bird steals its meal. The impact is normally enough to crack the shell and expose the soft flesh within.

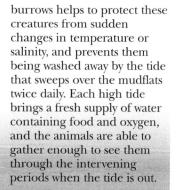

▲ An oystercatcher is skilled at detecting the rippled depressions in the mud that indicate a buried cockle. These large waders also feed on mussels and earthworms, but very rarely eat oysters.

◄ The two shells of a cockle are held shut by a powerful muscle. The oystercatcher cuts the muscle with its bill to make the shell gape open.

bacteria do not need oxygen, so they thrive in the deeper, airless levels of the mud.

In the quieter reaches of the estuary, the mud is populated by burrowing marine worms and molluscs. These are able to survive in the airless conditions by drawing oxygenated, food-bearing water into their burrows or siphon tubes from above the mud at high tide. Living in

burrows helps to protect these creatures from sudden changes in temperature or salinity, and prevents them being washed away by the tide that sweeps over the mudflats twice daily. Each high tide brings a fresh supply of water containing food and oxygen, and the animals are able to gather enough to see them through the intervening periods when the tide is out.

DANGER!
Extreme caution is necessary on mudflats. Go with a knowledgeable guide and tread carefully and slowly – the mud may be too soft to support your weight. Make sure tide times have been checked and someone on shore knows where you are going. Wrap up warm, as many mudflats are exposed to cold winds.

▲ Knot occur in vast numbers, often many thousands, on a few large, undisturbed mudflats. These medium-sized waders form single-species flocks from September until April.

◄ Although a relative newcomer to Britain, the elegant little egret is now a regular sight on mudflats on most estuaries in southern England.

► Mud shrimps spend much of their lives inside U-shaped burrows in the mud. Although they are hidden from view they are easily found by waders.

The upper surface of the mudflat often has a greenish gold bloom, seen at its best in bright sunlight. This is caused by millions of microscopic organisms, mainly single-celled algae called diatoms. These are able to make food using the energy of sunlight, like plants. They are a very important source of food for grazing molluscs, such as the tiny laver spire shell *Hydrobia ulvae*. This miniature marine snail is often so abundant on mudflats that the mud surface appears to be covered with a scattering of rice grains.

Hydrobia snails are, in turn, the principal source of food for the handsome shelduck – a species that feeds mainly on mudflats for most of the year. Its broad bill has serrated margins that function like strainers, enabling it to sift through the mud and filter out the snails as it sweeps its head from side to side. When the tide is in, *Hydrobia* are also preyed upon by crabs and bottom-living fish.

Hidden feeders

When the incoming tide floods the mudflat, the 'bloom' of microscopic algae on the mud surface is also harvested by the mud-dwelling animals that stay hidden in their burrows at low tide.

They include the peppery furrow shell, a common bivalve (two-shelled) mollusc that maintains contact with the mud surface via two very long, flexible siphon tubes. One siphon is long enough to sweep over the mud, drawing in food particles along with a current of water. The creature pumps the water through its gills to extract the oxygen and in the process removes any food particles. It then pumps the water back to the surface through the shorter siphon.

► Eelgrass grows on the higher reaches of mudflats where the mud is more stable. It is an important food source for Brent geese in autumn and winter.

Immense numbers of peppery furrow shells live buried in the mud. The only clues to their presence are tiny holes on the surface of the mudflat and faint traces of the sweep marks made by their siphons. Yet many wading birds can detect them, and long-billed species, such as the curlew, may be able to probe deeply enough into the mudflat to catch them.

Another animal that lives in a similar way is the Baltic tellin. This small bivalve mollusc is named for its abundance in the Baltic Sea, where salt levels are low. Its tolerance of brackish conditions enables it to flourish in the upper reaches of large estuaries, where the water salinity is too low for many marine molluscs. The huge quantities of delicate, pastel-coloured tellin shells that are washed up on the shore show how plentiful it is.

On many estuaries the smooth surface of the mud is covered by the coiled casts of the lugworm, one of the most common animals of tidal mudflats. Each lugworm lives in a U-shaped burrow with a depression at one end and a spiral of sand

▲ The ragworm is a common animal of estuarine mudflats. It crawls over and through the sediment in search of prey, which it seizes in its strong jaws.

► A young shelduck sifts the mud for molluscs. Shelducks start to return to Britain in October after their annual moult in tidal estuaries on the German coast.

▲ As they walk across the mud in search of food, waders leave their footprints behind them. The prints of several species can often be found together and even identified.

Tracks in the mud

At low tide, the safer upper reaches of mudflats provide many clues to the activities of the resident and visiting animals. It is easy to recognise some of the more obvious of these, and gain an insight into the sheer volume of life supported by this bleak-looking, yet rich, habitat.

◀ Lugworm casts are a common sight on mudflats. The nearby funnel-like depressions mark the location of each worm's head within its burrow.

▲ Waders often leave evidence of their feeding activities. Bill marks in the mud reveal where they have probed for invertebrate prey.

and mud at the other. Large lugworms lie beyond the reach of most predators, but long-billed godwits and curlews are often able to pluck them from their tunnels.

The silt-laden waters of an estuary prevent light from penetrating to any depth, so green plants and seaweeds are rarely able to survive in deeper water. The mud also provides an insecure anchorage, especially in channels where the ebbing tide flows quickly. A few seaweeds grow on the shallower flats, where fresh water trickles over the mud. They include gutweed, so named because its inflated tubular fronds resemble lengths of intestine. Eelgrass,

a true flowering plant, grows in the shallows on some mudflats, giving way to saltmarsh plants, such as glasswort and cord grass, near the high-tide line.

Seasonal visitors

In autumn, tens of thousands of waders, wildfowl and gulls arrive on the estuaries of Britain, having migrated from the Arctic and colder parts of Europe where they breed in summer. They are attracted by the mild Atlantic climate and the plentiful supply of food on the mud, as well as safe roosts on the nearby marshes.

Smaller waders such as dunlin form huge flocks at the water's edge, where their

burrowing prey comes up towards the surface to feed. Larger, longer-legged redshank, greenshank and godwits feed in the shallows. In a few favoured estuaries elegant avocets sweep their curved bills through shallow water in search of tiny shrimps. Lapwing, ringed plover, grey plover and knot run over the exposed mud looking for tiny molluscs, crustaceans and worms, while big, long-billed curlews stalk across the flat, searching for larger prey, such as crabs.

As the tide rises, feeding waders are concentrated along the water's edge. At intervals they take to the air in a flurry to move to higher ground.

WILDLIFE WATCH

Where can I see mudflats?

● In the south-west, fine mudflats can be seen on the Hayle, Tamar, Exe and Severn estuaries.

● Langstone Harbour and nearby Pagham Harbour on the south coast support huge numbers of waders and wildfowl in winter.

● The Wash in East Anglia is one of Britain's most important sites for waders in late autumn and winter. The Thames Estuary also has huge areas of mud that are vital to waders and wildfowl.

● In Wales and the north of England, the Dee Estuary, Morecambe Bay, the Humber Estuary and Budle Bay are all prime sites.

● Good Scottish sites include the mudflats of the Solway Estuary and Aberlady Bay.

● Strangford Lough in Northern Ireland has particularly fine tidal mudflats that attract large numbers of birds.

Coastal harbours

The quiet waters and surroundings of fishing ports and harbours provide permanent homes for a surprising range of animals and plants. Such places often resound with the cries of gulls and other seabirds, drawn by the promise of plentiful food.

From bustling fishing ports to abandoned quays on remote coasts, harbours are often rich in wildlife. They offer a combination of sheltered conditions and diverse habitats that suits a wide variety of native animals and plants. Many are also colonised by exotic species that have travelled from distant ports in the cargoes of visiting ships, or in the ballast that ships discharge.

For thousands of years the inlets and coves of Britain's coastline have provided protection from high winds and raging seas for ships, boats and their crews. A natural harbour was a huge asset to a coastal community, offering shelter for fishing boats and the chance to engage in profitable trade.

The larger and deeper the harbour, the bigger the ships it could accommodate – and the fatter the potential profits. Local engineers therefore sought to improve on the natural shelter provided by the bays and coves, by building sea defences and harbour walls. Entire communities were often involved in the construction of rough rock breakwaters, laboriously gathering the boulders, transporting them and laying them out. Hundreds of little fishing ports and harbours were created in this way, and flourished in the years when fishing was a major industry and ships were the most efficient means of carrying freight in coastal regions.

Many of these havens are now little used, except by yachts and other small leisure craft. Most of the fishing fleets have gone and road traffic is now the main form of transport. Yet the harbours survive and the shelter they provide is still valued by marine wildlife.

Man-made reefs

Below the tide line, a rocky breakwater forms an artificial reef. The outer, exposed wall is dominated by animals adapted to life on turbulent rocky shores. Bright red beadlet anemones and snakelock anemones cling to every surface, wafting their tentacles in the swirling current to catch food. Fish such as wrasse and blennies lurk in the fissures between the giant boulders, while shoals of large bass lunge at the tiny creatures dislodged by the pounding surf.

On the inner, sheltered side of the breakwater, the rocks are thick with sediment. Shore crabs and butterfish scavenge among the debris.

◀ **Herring gulls are to be found in all harbours. Immature birds like this one watch their parents to learn the art of scavenging from heaps of fishing nets.**

▼ **The harbour at St Ives in Cornwall provides a safe haven from the westerly gales that sweep in from the Atlantic. The area is particularly interesting in autumn, when there are many different gulls and other seabirds to observe.**

CATCH OF THE DAY

In fishing ports, the wharf where the fish and crabs are unloaded is a good place to look for interesting marine life. The arrival of a crab boat is often marked by the noisy squabbling of hungry herring gulls, watching for the moment when the crew unload the pots. It is often possible to make out the pointed shape of a large spiny spider crab amid the jumble of shell and claws, or the broader carapace of an edible crab. Although both these species are commonly seen on the lower shore, the specimens caught in deeper water are often much bigger. A number of other species are occasionally caught in the pots, including young conger eels, lesser-spotted dogfish and starfish. Heaps of old fishing nets often contain desiccated skate eggs, while old marker buoys may still have goose barnacles or mussels clinging to them.

The edible crab is easily recognised by the 'pie-crust' margins of its broad carapace, which may be up to 20cm (8in) across in a big specimen.

Lobster pots and crab pots catch a whole range of species that live in moderately deep water and are not commonly found on tidal shores.

▲ Dense colonies of mussels often develop on submerged harbour structures, but they thrive only where the water is silt-free and relatively unpolluted.

Small flounders lie on the bottom, camouflaged by the cryptic patterns on their skins, and shoals of tiny smelt flicker through the still shallows. Large grey mullet may be seen nosing around the outlets of freshwater streams, which are often thick with bright green *Enteromorpha* seaweed, often known as gutweed.

In the muddy sands of the harbour bed, the exposed tips of siphon tubes indicate the presence of large bivalve molluscs called peppery furrow shells, buried 10–20cm (4–8in) beneath the sand. Other, more specialised marine molluscs burrow into the timber of harbour piles and old wooden-hulled boats. Known as shipworms, they leave telltale holes and

galleries in the old timbers. It may even be possible to find live specimens in stacks of driftwood.

Harbour gulls

Harbours are among the most rewarding places to watch gulls. In fishing ports the regular passage of fishing boats provides easy pickings for these opportunists, and any fish scraps and offal tipped overboard are eagerly consumed by a number of species. Great flocks of hungry birds may follow the vessels for

▶ Rock samphire is normally found on rocky shores. However, it can also thrive on the stone breakwaters that are built to protect artificial harbours.

Ballan wrasse and other rocky shore fish find rich pickings in many harbours. They are most common in ports used by fishing vessels, since the boats are reliable sources of fish offal and other scraps.

UNUSUAL STOWAWAYS

Every year, some unusual visitors are accidentally transported to Britain's shores. Most of these animal stowaways are stray individuals that have found their way into bulk cargo. Tree frogs, spiders, geckos and other alien species have been discovered among bunches of bananas from the tropics, for example. Many die in transit through lack of food or cold, and many others cannot survive more than a few days in the cool British climate. Some species, however, have been imported from regions with climates similar to of Britain's, and in such

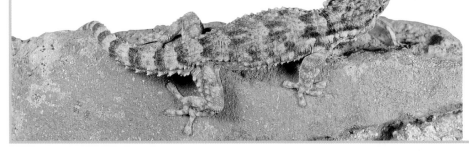

◄ Tree frogs have made the long crossing from Central and South America in boxes of bananas. Any insects in the same crate are unlikely to survive the journey!

numbers that they have been able to gain a foothold in native wildlife communities. Bulk imports of grain and seed can contain huge numbers of potentially damaging introductions. Grain weevils and the tiny larvae of micro-moths are frequently discovered in a variety of imported seed. This sort of accidental introduction led to outbreaks of Dutch elm disease in

▲ Scorpions living in Britain are at the mercy of seasonal weather. Nevertheless, colonies of the harmless *Euscorpius flavicaudus* have survived in the sheltered conditions of some southern harbours.

the 1970s, when bark beetle carrying the disease arrived in foreign timber.

Other stowaways seem to have had little effect on local ecology. For several years, for example, colonies of the small scorpion *Euscorpius flavicaudus* – from the Mediterranean – have lived largely undetected in the cracks of warm, south-facing walls in larger south coast ports.

◄ The Moorish or wall gecko is a southern European and North African species that occasionally turns up in crates of fruit.

◄ Sargasso weed, an alien floating seaweed, has been accidentally introduced to several harbours. In some areas it grows so thickly that it can impede the passage of boats.

◄ Young kittiwakes may remain in the vicinity of harbours throughout the autumn and winter.

the glaucous gull but is much smaller. A far rarer find is the ivory gull. No bird-lover could fail to be impressed by a close encounter with this beautiful silky white bird, which will have travelled from the Arctic to reach British shores.

In the south, autumn gales carry Mediterranean species north to Britain, including the aptly named Mediterranean gull. Strong Atlantic gales may bring in birds that are sighted even more rarely, such as the North American ring-billed gull, Bonaparte's gull and laughing gull, although identifying these vagrants takes patience and practice.

Dainty kittiwakes often breed near harbours in noisy cliff colonies. At the end of the season adults move out to sea, but young birds may stay to feed in harbours through the autumn and winter. They are distinguished by a black zigzag pattern on their upper wings – although Sabine's gull, a rare autumn visitor to western shores, looks similar.

hundreds of miles out at sea, then return with them to their home ports. Among these, some unusual or rare visitors may be seen. In northern harbours it may be possible to spot the stocky glaucous gull. This Arctic bird moves south in late autumn and is distinguished from herring gulls, common gulls and black-headed gulls by its great size and its lack of black wing tips.

Another autumn and winter visitor to northern ports is the Iceland gull, which resembles

◄ Red valerian is such a feature of harbours in Devon and Cornwall that it has been called 'Padstow pride'. It flowers well into October, providing food for late-flying butterflies and bees.

Where the waves break against the more exposed parts of the harbour, purple sandpipers and turnstones skitter back and forth with each surge and crash, watching for morsels of food brought in by the surf. Cormorants also enter harbours in search of tiny flatfish and eels. They swim low in the water, their backs awash, and often only their heads and snake-like necks are visible above the surface as they pause between diving to hunt on the harbour bed.

Grey seals frequently come close to small western ports, and may be seen as they surface for air. In many Scottish harbours the seals have become so used to fishing boats that they swim into the still, shallow harbour waters in search of food.

Local colour

Several salt-tolerant plants colonise harbour walls and breakwaters above the zones that are regularly drenched by the waves. Thrift, buckshorn plantain, wild cabbage, sea beet and rock samphire grow side by side on some breakwaters. More sheltered crevices may house colonies of navelwort and polypody fern.

The bright blooms of red valerian form eye-catching displays around the harbours of the south-west. The plant is

an introduction from the Mediterranean and flourishes in warm, sheltered conditions. The strong aniseed scent and feathery foliage of fennel grace many harbours, and the cracks in old walls may reveal the straggling stems of thyme-leaved sandwort.

Alien invaders

A few exotic plants have managed to cross the open oceans to become an established part of the local ecology. They include the smooth cord-grass that was accidentally introduced to Southampton from North America some time before 1870. It formed a hybrid with the native cord-grass, and the hybrid form was so vigorous that it rapidly took over large areas of mud in sheltered harbours and estuaries.

The seeds of smooth cord-grass were brought to Britain in ballast water, taken on by ships to keep them stable in rough seas. Sargasso weed and Japanese wakame – both marine algae, or seaweeds – were introduced to harbours in a similar way. Like hybrid cord-grass these exotic seaweeds may become a problem, since they spread rapidly, vitually nothing eats them and they are almost impossible to destroy.

▲ In autumn and winter, Atlantic gales may sometimes bring in rare vagrant gulls. One of these, the laughing gull, can be identified by its long drooping bill and tapered silhouette.

◄ Coastal flowers are often able to find a roothold in the most tenuous of sites around the harbour. The daisy-like flowers of sea mayweed can be seen as late as September.

▲ The black or ship rat was once the scourge of ports. It is now one of the rarest British mammals, restricted to a few major harbours and islands.

▼ Inquisitive grey seals may venture into harbours during the autumn months, attracted by the sheltered waters and plentiful fish.

WILDLIFE WATCH

Where can I see harbour wildlife?

● Many fishermen will let you take a look in their nets or lobster pots to see crabs, starfish and baby conger eels.

● Harbours often have small marine aquariums that are stocked with local species. These offer a chance to get a close look at the animals that live in and around the harbour.

● Time your visit to see the harbour at low tide, which usually reveals plenty that is of interest. Check the tide tables to select a good day and time. Local papers often give details of high and low tides.

Rocky shores

Forged from hard stone by the relentless power of the sea and the daily rhythm of the tides, the rocky shore is a violent, ever-shifting frontier. Despite its hazards, it is home to a diverse mix of wildlife.

The shoreline of the British Isles is one of the longest and most varied in Europe. The southern and eastern coasts are dominated by sandy beaches, shingle ridges and tidal mudflats, deposited and constantly shifted by the swirling currents of the English Channel and the North Sea. By contrast, the northern and western coasts are buttressed against the might of the Atlantic Ocean by cliffs and ridges of hard rocks such as granite and basalt, as well as ancient sandstone. This has created rugged rocky shores that are relentlessly eroded by pounding waves.

These rocky shores have been shaped by millions of years of such erosion. Waves surging into narrowing cracks and gullies blast the rock apart with explosive force. Where the sea penetrates seams of softer rock it rapidly excavates more deeply, shaping the hundreds of sheltered bays that punctuate the jagged western coasts from Dorset to the Hebrides. Rain and wind add to the processes of erosion, slowly smoothing the ragged edges of the newly fractured rocks and washing away sediments from the softer cliff faces. Between the bays, the cliffs and stacks of ragged headlands overlook rocky reefs that are submerged at high tide. Constantly scoured by swirling currents, both the shores and submerged reefs provide habitats for a wonderful variety of highly specialised animals.

Sea watch

A rocky shore can be a formidable place to visit in autumn and winter, when gale-force winds whip spray high into the air and drive it across headlands and promontories. The wind and salt spray effectively prune the blackthorn and other hardy shrubs that grow on the headlands, wind-cutting them into stunted and sometimes strangely contorted forms. Despite these conditions, the headlands that frame a rocky bay can provide ideal vantage points from which to see animals and birds.

A variety of ocean birds that are not usually seen from the shore are often driven closer to the coast by windy, rough conditions on the open sea. A careful search with binoculars may reveal the fluttering flight of a tiny storm petrel, or a group of Manx shearwaters, their flashing wings switching from black to white as the birds swoop and bank over the waves.

▶ A gannet is a spectacular sight whether resting or flying. These birds favour rocky sloping cliffs from which they can launch into space and catch rising air currents.

The crashing waves and twice-daily rise and fall of the tides have a profound influence on the wildlife of rocky shores, creating several distinct zones of animals and plants at each level of the tidal shore.

Gannets, which usually feed far out to sea, often patrol the upwelling currents of rocky headlands in autumn in search of shoaling fish driven to the surface by feeding bottle-nosed dolphins or harbour porpoises. Even from a distance, these massive white birds with their black wing tips are unmistakable as they cruise high above the water, fold their wings and plummet into the waves. Very large shoals of fish can trigger feeding frenzies as dozens of gannets home in and plunge repeatedly into the sea amid a swirling mass of frightened fish and regularly surfacing dolphins. Great black-backed gulls, kittiwakes and fulmars are usually quick to join the fray and pick off any injured or disoriented fish left near the surface.

Large colonies of kittiwakes are commonly seen around the coasts until autumn, when the majority of adults leave to spend the winter at sea.

Beach litter

High above the tide line a litter of broken crab or urchin shells are clues to the feeding habits of gulls and crows, which drop the shells to break them and reveal the soft flesh within. On deserted beaches in northern Scotland, however, the same type of debris can indicate the feeding activity of a resident otter, which often brings its catch ashore to eat.

BREEDING SEALS

Grey seals can often be seen close to rocky shores as they bob about beyond the surf, waiting for the tide to ebb before hauling themselves out on to rocks or stony beaches.

During the autumn breeding season – which lasts from September to December – they use similar sites, favouring the most inaccessible, sheltered bays or uninhabited islands just offshore. Each big bull seal defends an area of shore around a harem of females, noisily warning off any rivals. Each female has a single pup, which is born high above the tide line and suckled for about three weeks. The growing pups are quite vocal, and their howling and barking, echoing off the cliffs that surround them, can sometimes be heard over great distances.

About 80 per cent of the European population of grey seals breeds around the coasts of the British Isles. Some of the largest breeding colonies are centred on the islands of western Wales, such as Ramsey Island, and on the Farne Islands in north-east England. These autumn colonies offer some of the best opportunities for watching grey seals.

In the north, around the many sheltered coves and inlets of the Scottish islands, and in eastern England, where the rocky shores give way to large expanses of sandy beach, the grey seal's range overlaps that of the common or harbour seal. This is smaller and less robust-looking than the grey seal, with a shorter snout and a more rounded head. It prefers shallow, sheltered inlets to the more exposed waters inhabited by its cousin, so is not so characteristic of rocky shores.

▲ Grey seals occur off most of Britain's coasts. They spend much of their year at sea, but in early autumn they return to secluded shingle coves, islands or similar sites to breed.

◄ Common seals are actually less common than grey seals, especially on rocky shores, but they can sometimes be seen basking in the autumn sun on seaweed-covered rocks close to deep water.

Lower on the shore, but above the normal high tide mark, lie mounds of rotting seaweed or marine algae, thrown up by storms and the highest tides. These attract swarms of kelp flies, which lay their eggs among the decaying fronds. The flies and their larvae provide rich pickings for rock pipits – small, streaky brown wagtail-like birds that descend from the cliffs to forage among the boulders of the lower shore. The dead fish, shattered crabs and other edible debris on the strand line also attract terrestrial scavengers, such as rats, foxes and crows.

Once thought to be a rare visitor to British and Irish coasts, the leopard spotted goby is now known to be a common resident of shallow waters, although it is not found on the North Sea coast of England.

MARITIME PLANTS

The cliffs and slopes above the tidal zones of rocky shores are hostile habitats for seaweeds and plants. The land is too dry for seaweeds, but since it is regularly drenched with salt spray thrown up by the waves or carried on the wind, it is too salty and exposed for most land plants.

Such slopes are colonised by specialist maritime plants, such as wild carrot, sea plantain and thrift. These plants are able to cope with the conditions, and although they grow sparsely they are able to take over large areas of rock because they have no competition from more vigorous but less salt-tolerant plants that grow above the spray zone.

The exposed rock faces also support maritime lichens such as the bright orange *Caloplaca* and yellow or orange *Xanthoria*. Black tar spot lichen grows closest to the tide line, forming long dark bands around rocky bays and headlands.

▲ The rocks in the splash zone, just above the high-water mark, are often colonised by lichens. They include *Xanthoria parietina*, which encrusts rocks in irregular patches of colour.

◀ A characteristic maritime plant of rocky shores, thrift can grow in any available crevice and blooms well into October.

Natural zones
The rocky ledges that are regularly swept by the rising tide are dominated by several species of leathery brown algae known as wracks. Each is able to tolerate a different degree of exposure to the air, so they form distinct zones along the shore.

High up on the beach lie the dark greenish or orange-brown fronds of channelled wrack. Each frond is inrolled along its length to help conserve water during the long hours between the highest tides. Lower down, the shore is dominated by the olive green fronds of spiral or flat wrack.

Lower still, around the mid-water mark, the paler olive green or brown fronds of bladder wrack begin to appear. The bubble-like gas bladders that give it the alternative name of 'popweed' enable its heavy, leathery fronds to float upright in shallow water. In very sheltered conditions much of the middle shore may be dominated by the luxuriant fronds of egg or knotted wrack, with its sultana-like fruiting bodies and large, single bladders.

The toothed fronds of serrated or toothed wrack can be seen only around the low-tide mark, or in deep rock pools. Less leathery than many other seaweeds, this species is unable to survive long periods out of the water.

Rock pools
When the tide is at its lowest, it exposes huge expanses of seaweeds. Tiny cushion stars – and occasionally larger species such as the spiny starfish, which can be up to 80cm (30in) across – may be left stranded among the seaweeds by the retreating tide. Other animals that normally live among the seaweeds find refuge in rock pools.

The character of rock pools varies according to their level on the shore. The pools of the lower shore are the richest in marine life, since they spend the shortest time exposed to the sun and air, and are less likely to heat up and dry out. Prawns can often be spotted darting for cover when they are alarmed by moving

The broad fronds of spiral wrack can often be found on the upper shore. Their heavy, swollen, pod-like reproductive tips form distinctive clusters and are easy to recognise.

shadows. By contrast shannies, being curious little fish by nature, often emerge from beneath seaweed or rocks to inspect the toes of anyone wading in a deep pool.

In shallow water the rock surfaces are often encrusted with bright pink coralline algae and beds of filamentous red and green seaweeds that teem with small marine life. Crevices between boulders provide hiding places for a variety of species, including

crabs such as the broad-clawed and long-clawed porcelain crabs. The worm pipefish – a relative of the sea horse – is common on the lower shore, although so well camouflaged that it is rarely seen.

Flood tide

As the tide rises, corkwing wrasse swim into the shallows to take advantage of the feast of animals dislodged by wave action. In early autumn greater pipefish come together to breed, and move inshore where they can be seen skulking beneath seaweeds waiting for mates.

In deeper water, large fronds of kelp buoyed up by the rising tide are surrounded by big wrasse, such as the green or red Ballan wrasse, searching for molluscs and crustaceans to eat. The fronds themselves are covered with much smaller animals such as the electric blue and glowing gold sea slug *Facelina coronata*, which glides over the surface of the fronds looking for prey. Blue-rayed limpets and chitons cling to the rocks among the root-like holdfasts of the kelp. Sessile jellyfish anchor themselves to the edges of the fronds, their clusters of tentacles sifting tiny particles from the gently swirling currents. Compared with the exposure of low tide, it is a different world.

▲ The rock pipit occurs on all coasts except those of south-east England. It feeds on rocky beaches, where it hunts for insects and other small creatures among beached seaweeds.

◄ Brittlestars may sometimes be found wedged in small spaces in rock pools, or beneath boulders. Their delicate arms are sometimes tangled together in apparently inextricable knots.

◄ The long stinging tentacles of the snakelocks anemone gather tiny organisms for food. Unlike many anemones it cannot retract its tentacles, so on rocky shores it lives only in pools that never dry out at low tide.

▼ A rocky shore is a harsh habitat, subject to more extremes than any other natural environment. Yet even the most exposed, ragged rocks – such as these on the Llŷn coast in Gwynedd, Wales – support a wide variety of marine wildlife.

WILDLIFE WATCH

How can I see rocky shore wildlife?

● To get the best out of a visit to a rocky shore, aim to get there a couple of hours before low tide. Adopt the strategy of beachcombing birds such as the rock pipit and follow the tide as it recedes down the shore, to discover the various animals that have been stranded.

● High-level coastal paths along many rocky coastlines offer excellent opportunities for viewing birds and marine mammals on the shore below or out at sea. If possible, take a pair of binoculars. From a distance, it is also easier to see the distinct pattern of zones on the shore.

● Remember – if you turn over boulders or seaweeds, always replace them afterwards to protect the creatures that are living beneath them.

● For information on how you can help to look after coastal habitats contact the Marine Conservation Society, Unit 3, Wolf Business Park, Alton Road, Ross-on-Wye, Herefordshire, HR9 5NB, (telephone 01989 566017) or visit www.mcsuk.org

The shingle outpost of Dungeness

The windswept plains of Dungeness form one of the wildest corners of the south coast. A huge expanse of shingle dotted with maritime flowers and wind-stunted scrub, it is the unlikely refuge of many different birds and insects.

The largest shingle headland in Europe, Dungeness juts out into the English Channel from the coast of Kent in south-east England. Compared to the comfortable farms, orchards and hop gardens to be found inland, its harsh, elemental character is almost shocking, and at first it seems like a stony desert devoid of life. The landscape has been created by wind and sea, and most of the buildings that dot this bleak region look as if the wind and sea could sweep them away overnight.

The wildness of Dungeness is part of its attraction, however, and certainly does nothing to discourage the wildlife that makes the place so special. A number of plants have adapted to withstand the salt winds, and Dungeness is one of Britain's premier locations for both migrant and breeding birds. Rare species may be seen there in autumn and the flooded gravel pits teem with birds in summer. Dungeness is also, perhaps surprisingly, a prime site for spotting unusual moths.

Altogether, Dungeness covers some 850 hectares (2000 acres). Much of this area is managed as a nature reserve by the Royal Society for the Protection of Birds (RSPB). It forms the seaward tip of the much larger low-lying area known generally as Romney Marsh, although the region also includes Walland Marsh and extends inland as the Rother Levels. On bright, sunny days, the grazing marshes that lie on the landward side of the shingle glitter with the waters of innumerable drainage channels. In late autumn the marshes attract large numbers of lapwings and golden plovers for the winter, plus smaller numbers of ruff. During the last 50 years some parts of the marsh have been deep-drained for cereal growing and red-legged partridges feed on the fertile ploughed land.

Tidal deposits

Some 4000 years ago, the great expanse of shingle and alluvial soil that now make up Dungeness and Romney Marsh did not exist, and the area was a broad, shallow bay.

The original coastline of the bay can still be traced, extending through the town of Appledore more than 18km (11 miles) inland from the tip of Dungeness. Shingle swept along the coast by the sea has created the broad spit of Dungeness, while silt carried downstream by the River Rother has infilled the area behind the shingle to create the flat alluvial marshland.

The sea continually dumps new shingle on the beaches of Dungeness. Over time, storm waves and high tides build this up into high ridges, and new beaches form on their seaward flanks. The process has created a series of ridges that resemble the contour lines on a map, charting the growth of the spit over the centuries.

A male red-backed shrike adds to his larder. Surplus food items are impaled on thorns to be eaten later.

Sooty shearwaters pass Dungeness in small numbers in early autumn. Although they are sometimes seen close to land, a telescope will usually give a better view.

This movement of the shingle – known as longshore drift – also carries it around the foreland from west to east, so for hundreds of years the spit has been very slowly moving eastwards. This natural movement to the east is now artificially counteracted by scooping up shingle from the eastern side and dumping it back on the south-western side. Gravel extraction in the past has created a series of pits inland from the sea. Now abandoned and flooded, they attract a variety of waterbirds and form the heart of the RSPB reserve.

Dungeness's nuclear power station dominates the southern shore. Further inland, disused and flooded gravel pits provide a haven for many coastal plants and animals.

Shifting land

Shingle banks are among the most unstable and hostile of all plant habitats, and only a few highly specialised plants such as sea kale can grow on them. This wild cabbage forms large clumps on the higher, drier banks away from the sea. Dungeness has one of the largest concentrations of sea kale in Britain – the species is now scarce elsewhere.

In early autumn, the bright flowers of yellow horned-poppy can still be seen, although many of the blooms will have given way to the elongated seed pods that are a distinctive feature of the plant. Sea pea, curled dock, viper's-bugloss, ragwort and early scurvy grass are common on the Dungeness shingle. Many are prolific seed producers and provide autumn food for flocks of greenfinches, linnets and goldfinches.

Dungeness is an important site for several unusual plants such as Nottingham catchfly, marsh cinquefoil, upright chickweed, bulbous meadow-grass and yellow vetch – another species that is rare in other parts of the country.

Further away from the sea the shingle is more stable, and where it gradates into the marsh it supports broad

stretches of grass punctuated by brambles, gorse and wind-stunted elder and sallow. This low scrub may not look very welcoming, but it is a vital

▶ Glasswort can grow on salt-laden silt and cope with regular flooding by the sea at high water. It grows on quieter patches of tidal mud at Dungeness.

MARSH FROG

The pools and drainage ditches of Dungeness and Romney Marsh are home to the marsh frog, a continental species that is now quite common in the area. The population has grown from a group of just 12 individuals released on the fringe of Romney Marsh in 1935.

Larger than the common frog, it can be distinguished by its more pointed snout, and the male's inflatable vocal sacs.

Marsh frogs are cautious and rather wary animals. However, they do like to sit on floating vegetation or waterside banks to sunbathe.

Among the most conspicuous migrant insects are painted lady butterflies, which can often be seen sipping nectar from wayside flowers.

COMINGS AND GOINGS

At Dungeness the autumn migration starts in late July and continues until November. When easterly winds blow, they bring 'drift migrants' such as wrynecks, red-backed shrikes and icterine warblers, swept off-track on their way south to the tropics. In late September many winter visitors arrive from northern Europe, such as the flocks of fieldfares and redwings that pass overhead. On some days the bushes can be alive with tiny goldcrests, which are often accompanied by their rarer relative, the firecrest.

In spring, the best time to see migrant birds is when southerly winds are blowing. Ideal conditions would be clear weather to the south, but with a belt of rain or cloud cover over Dungeness to hamper the birds' progress north and encourage them to land. On

◀ Swallows pass through Dungeness in both autumn and spring. They breed in Britain during the summer and fly south in October to spend the winter in Africa, south of the Sahara.

clear, sunny days there are fewer birds about, because most simply fly straight past without pausing.

Ring ouzels, chiffchaffs and wheatears are the first birds to make landfall in March, and during April large numbers of willow warblers pass through. The stream of migrants becomes a flood in May when the swallows arrive,

skimming low over the waves, and the regular chats, flycatchers and warblers are joined by rarities such as the golden oriole, hoopoe and serin. These three species are all birds that live mainly in southern Europe, but they arrive at south-coast sites, including Dungeness, when they overshoot their target and fly well beyond their usual breeding range.

Every year a few birds arrive at Dungeness that are extreme rarities in Britain and October is one of the most likely times to see them. Previous records have included waders from North America, such as the least sandpiper and lesser yellowlegs. Other visitors have

▲ The fieldfare is a winter-visiting thrush that arrives from late autumn. These birds often settle to rest before flying inland to feed on fruiting trees such as hawthorn.

come from the east, such as the dusky warbler, black-throated thrush and Caspian tern. In spring, birds from Europe may mistakenly cross the Channel as they head north. These vagrants often include the odd woodchat shrike. Much rarer are short-toed treecreepers, great spotted cuckoos and collared pratincoles, all of which have been seen at Dungeness in recent years.

◀ The exotic-looking hoopoe occasionally appears at Dungeness in the autumn, although it is more likely to be seen in spring. It uses its long bill to probe the ground for invertebrates.

▶ A close relative of woodpeckers, the wryneck is a secretive visitor that is seen mainly in the autumn. It often feeds on the ground and favours ants.

refuge for the small migrant birds that arrive in spring after an exhausting cross-channel flight.

Migrant birds

Dungeness is the perfect place for watching bird migration. In both autumn and spring, an extraordinary variety of waterbirds, landbirds and seabirds stream past, travelling to and from their wintering grounds. In autumn, poor weather and high winds

blowing in off the sea can lead to the appearance of several seabirds that are not normally seen from the shore. These can include Leach's storm petrels, sooty shearwaters or perhaps even a diminutive grey phalarope.

Spring can be equally exciting – on some days hundreds or even thousands of wildfowl, waders, gulls and terns are on the move. Among the most unusual of these spring migrants are the pomarine skuas that pass in

early May, flying north from their winter home in the open Atlantic to breed in Russia.

The southern shore of Dungeness is dominated by the towering bulk of the nuclear power station, built right next to the sea. The power station's cooling system generates an outflow of warm water, and the place where this enters the sea – known to birdwatchers as 'The Patch' – attracts masses of seabirds throughout the year. They include several species of gulls, as well as a variety of terns.

The rare stinking hawk's-beard, named for its distinctive smell, grows only on the shingle at Dungeness. It died out in 1980, but has been reintroduced.

Yellow horned-poppy is one of the most striking shingle plants to be found at Dungeness. Its bright flowers can be seen from June to September.

Most are common species, but mixed in with them may be a little gull, perhaps a party of black terns, an Arctic tern or even a roseate tern. In late summer and autumn, passing Arctic skuas and great skuas regularly stop off at The Patch to harry the feeding gulls.

Barely a stone's throw from the power station lies the Dungeness Bird Observatory, set up to monitor the migrant birds that fly through the site. Large numbers of birds are ringed and recorded by the

Constantly shifting shingle is an unforgiving habitat for plants. However, specialised plants soon colonise the more stable landward side of shingle ridges.

observatory staff and helpers. Wooden constructions – known as Heligoland traps – are built over bushes to channel birds into a catching box. Extra-fine 'mist nets' strung across clearings in the trapping area are also used. The ensnared birds are ringed and released, and their details contribute to a mass of data that both helps conservation and assists in unravelling the complexities of migration.

Flooded pits
By late autumn the flooded gravel pits on Dungeness are starting to attract the many birds that will use them as feeding and roosting sites throughout the winter.

The best of these pits lie within the RSPB reserve. This is the society's oldest reserve, established in 1932 to protect shingle-nesting birds, especially terns and Kentish

▲ A few Mediterranean gulls breed amid the colonies of black-headed gulls. In breeding plumage they are distinguished by an entirely black head, a thicker, down-turned bill and all-white wing tips.

▶ Sea kale, with its broad fleshy leaves, thrives on the shingle. Cultivated varieties have edible asparagus-like shoots.

plovers, that were badly affected by fox predation and disturbance by people. Islands within the flooded pits now provide secure nesting areas for common terns and black-headed gulls in spring. Kentish plovers no longer breed here and neither do the Sandwich terns that, until very recently, nested here in a large colony. There are other breeding rarities, however. The breeding colonies of black-headed gulls regularly attract a few pairs of the similar-looking Mediterranean gull. This species first nested in Britain in 1968 in a black-headed gull colony in Hampshire. Since then it has

bred at a number of localities in southern England, with Dungeness being one of its main strongholds.

The gravel pits are at their most interesting late in the year, when masses of ducks and grebes arrive. The smew, a scarce winter visitor to Britain, is regularly seen. The elegant black-and-white drakes are unmistakable. Smews feed mostly on fish and their bills have serrated edges to help them grip their slippery prey.

All five British species of grebe may be seen on Burrowes Pit in autumn and winter. The great crested and little grebe – the two most common species – may be

▲ Many brent geese feed at Dungeness from October to March, and even more pass through on migration in autumn and spring.

▲ Small numbers of smew, such as this male, may appear on the flooded gravel pits of Dungeness if mainland Europe is hit by hard winter weather.

joined by red-necked, Slavonian and black-necked grebes. Red-throated divers also appear there at times.

On the south-west side of the RSPB reserve an area of rough grazing known as Dengemarsh has been developed for birds. Shallow pools attract hundreds and sometimes thousands of

wigeon in late autumn and winter. The pools are also used by breeding redshanks and lapwings in spring. Recently established reedbeds are occupied by wintering bitterns and in recent years a continental species, the penduline tit, has become a regular winter visitor.

Visiting insects

While birds are the most conspicuous wild visitors to Dungeness, the area also attracts a variety of insects. Migrant dragonflies and particularly butterflies are

▶ Long-tailed ducks arrive in autumn to spend the winter on the Dungeness gravel pits. This male is in breeding plumage, acquired in late autumn.

▼ The flat expanse of pools, a legacy of commercial gravel extraction, is now overseen by the RSPB.

a feature of the summer and early autumn. Most prominent are painted lady butterflies and, in some years, clouded yellows. Both can be seen well into October.

Migrant moths are another big feature of Dungeness wildlife, including the spectacular convolvulus and oleander hawk-moths, and the day-flying hummingbird hawk-moth. Some of the smaller, more common species include the lackey moth, buff ermine, flounced rustic, and

the heart and dart moth. In some years the cinnabar moth can be common in late spring and early summer; its black and orange striped caterpillars live on the ragwort that grows on the shingle. Dungeness also has a number of spiders and beetles not found anywhere else in Britain.

Dungeness may not be the most scenic of landscapes, but there is nowhere to match it elsewhere in Europe. It is rich in wildlife and has a strange, haunting beauty of its own.

Places to visit in Dungeness

Among the areas protected by nature reserve status, Dungeness is the finest site in Britain for shingle habitats. A wide range of specialised shingle plants can be found here, including a number of rarities that are confined to this region. Rare species of insect also live at Dungeness and the site is used by large numbers of breeding birds. Owing to its location on the south coast, many birds arrive, some unexpectedly, during autumn and spring migrations.

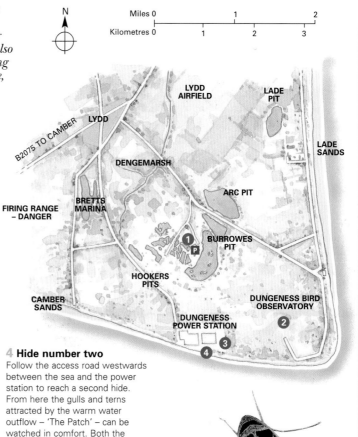

1 Dungeness RSPB Reserve

On the Lydd to Dungeness road, the RSPB Reserve is approximately 2.4km (1½ miles) from the Lydd roundabout on the B2075 Folkestone to Lydd road. It is well signposted. The reserve is open every day from nine o'clock in the morning until nine o'clock at night (or sunset if earlier). Admission is free for RSPB members, but there is an admission charge for non-members. The facilities are very good, with a number of hides overlooking the gravel pits that attract many of the birds. Up-to-date information about which birds are present is always available. A circular walk can be taken around the reserve. For details, telephone 01797 320 588, or email dungeness@rspb.org.uk.

2 The bird observatory

This can be reached by taking the road past the old lighthouse to the cottages at the end. The 'moat' – a dry depression full of bushes surrounding the cottages – is always worth inspecting for migrant birds. Also check the bushes around the old lighthouse and the expanse of gorse. The large patch of bushes to the north of the observatory is a trapping site. A number of paths cross it to allow people to explore the area. The bird observatory has basic hostel-type accommodation. For more information contact Dungeness Bird Observatory, 11 RNSSS, Dungeness, Kent, TN29 9NA (telephone 01797 321309) or email dungeness.obs@tinyonline.co.uk

3 Hide number one

At the eastern end of the power station a hide has been constructed on the beach from which to watch the passage of seabirds, wildfowl and waders in autumn and spring. It is even more rewarding to stand on the point itself, just to the north-east of the new lighthouse, but this is very exposed.

4 Hide number two

Follow the access road westwards between the sea and the power station to reach a second hide. From here the gulls and terns attracted by the warm water outflow – 'The Patch' – can be watched in comfort. Both the hides overlook the sea and are owned by the bird observatory. If they are locked, it will be necessary to collect a key from the observatory.

The stunning oleander hawk-moth is a scarce visitor, but arrives nearly every year in late summer and autumn. It was first recorded just along the coast at Dover in 1833.

WILDLIFE WATCH

When should I visit Dungeness?

● Dungeness offers wildlife interest throughout the year, although different seasons have their own highlights.

● Autumn is the best season for birdwatchers because, unless the weather is calm and settled, almost any migrant species could turn up.

● In winter, keep an eye open for wildfowl and hunting raptors.

● Spring is an exciting time, both for watching passage migrant birds and for seeing the arrival of breeding species including terns and gulls.

● In early summer, visitors can usually see young terns and gulls being fed by their parents. The return passage of migrant waders often begins as early as July, just when the specialised shingle flora is at its most colourful.

◄ **The gravel pits attract gulls, terns and a variety of waterfowl throughout the year.**

Animals and plants in focus

Waterside watch

- The water vole
- The great crested grebe
- Coots and moorhens
- Recognising geese
- The European eel

- White-clawed crayfish
- The pearl mussel
- Mosquitoes
- Water fleas
- Bulrushes and bur-reeds
- The balsams

The water vole

The bustling activity of the water vole is all too rarely seen today, but conservation efforts aimed at protecting this shy mammal are starting to produce a small recovery in numbers in wetland reserves and on river banks in towns and cities.

In recent years it has become an increasingly rare privilege to see a water vole swimming near the river bank or to hear the distinctive plop of one taking to the water. Numbers have decreased drastically in the last 15 years or so, down from an estimated 7.3 million in 1990 to just 875,000 in 1998, but the water vole population has been in decline for much longer than that. It may not be too late to reverse the situation, however. Water vole conservation is important and worthwhile, not just because these are attractive and harmless creatures, but because their continued presence is a valuable indicator of a healthy and viable waterside habitat.

Rarely found far from fresh water in Britain, the water vole is markedly less aquatic in continental Europe. Indeed, in parts of southern Central Europe, water voles behave more like moles, often living in pastures and other farmland, and excavating and living in burrows. This behaviour has led to the species being regarded as a pest in some areas.

Tunnel dwellers
Water voles normally live in an extensive system of burrows in river banks, inside which they construct nest chambers and line them with grass. A burrow system usually has at least one entrance below water level, which can be used without exposing the animal to view.

Water voles inhabit waterside areas with rich, varied vegetation, such as river banks and pond margins.

Until recently, water voles had no legal protection at all, but by 1998 their numbers had declined so much that the Wildlife and Countryside Act was revised to give them some legal protection. Although it is not illegal to trap and kill water voles, their burrows are now protected and they must not be disturbed in their homes. This means that river managers in particular are obliged by law to take account of this small mammal. They cannot, for example, permit waterside engineering works that might destroy water vole habitats and burrows through the use of heavy machinery.

WATER VOLE FACT FILE

The size of a small rat, this mammal lives near water and eats waterside vegetation. Its body and tail are covered in glossy brown fur, although a few black ones can be found in Scotland. Some water voles have a white tail tip or white patches on the forehead, body or feet.

● NAMES
Common names: water vole, water rat
Scientific name: *Arvicola terrestris*

● HABITAT
Beside lowland rivers, streams and ponds, often passes undetected in reedbeds; sometimes found in uplands, along urban rivers and on salt marshes

● DISTRIBUTION
Most of southern and central England, eastern and lowland Scotland, parts of Wales; also on the Isle of Wight and Anglesey, absent from the Isle of Man and Ireland

● STATUS
Population estimated at about 1.2 million; common in a few scattered areas; had declined to 875,000 by 1998

● SIZE
Length, head and body 14–22cm (5½–9in), tail 9–14cm (3½–5½in); weight 150–300g (5½–10½oz)

● KEY FEATURES
Chestnut brown silky fur, rounded face, snub nose, very small ears and thin dark tail; sexes similar

● HABITS
Often active in daylight as well as at night; swims in still or slow-flowing water; emerges to sit on haunches and nibble food held between paws

● VOICE
Usually silent, but when disturbed dives into the water with an audible plop

● FOOD
Wide range of plants especially grasses and sedges but also roots and bulbs and occasionally small animals such as fish

● BREEDING
Litter size generally 5; usually 3–4 litters per year, born March–October

● NEST
By the waterside, a burrow chamber or ball-shaped nest woven from stems of reeds, rushes or grasses. Built among dense tussocks where water table is high

● YOUNG
Fur darker, greyer and less glossy than adults' coat; weaned at 3 weeks

● SIGNS
Small groups of shiny, greenish, cylindrical droppings in latrines – areas of close-cropped grass, sometimes with small heaps of cropped vegetation; tiny star-shaped footprints in mud

An active water vole tends to be busy by day. Water voles like clean water and diverse vegetation, so evidence of a vole population suggests a healthy habitat.

Distribution map key

■	Present all year round
□	Not present

The ears are tiny, barely emerging from the fur.

Fur is thick, with long, glossy guard hairs that stand up when the vole is alarmed or excited, making the animal appear larger than normal.

Small, bright, beady eyes are set in an appealing, chubby face.

The front paws are dextrous enough to hold and manipulate food as it is eaten.

A water vole feeds on the tenderest parts of a waterside plant. These mainly vegetarian rodents are known to harvest summer grasses and store them in their burrows for later consumption.

Underwater swimmers

Most rodents are capable of swimming if they have to, but water voles are very much at home in the water. They take to it when alarmed, but they are by no means entirely safe there. Like most small aquatic animals and birds, water voles are vulnerable to attack from above and below. Their main predators are mink, stoats, herons and pike.

Water voles swim well and often dive, but not very deep. Their soft fur traps a layer of air close to the skin. Underwater, the pressure forces some air out, creating a trail of bubbles.

The vole has to visit the surface frequently to breathe, so it cannot remain submerged long enough to escape determined predators. However, a frightened animal will usually surface only under cover of vegetation where it cannot easily be seen.

In the breeding season the animals may spend 60 per cent of their time in the burrow, even more at other times of the year. Activity comes in bursts – at night as well as in the daytime – with a few hours rest in between.

Where burrowing is not possible, such as in reedbeds or areas of waterlogged soil, water voles may live among tussocky vegetation or weave rushes into a domed nest, about 30cm (12in) across.

Busy breeders

The young are born between March and September or even October after a pregnancy lasting around three weeks. Three or four litters may be produced in a season, with an average of five young in each. The blind, hairless babies weigh about 5g (¼oz) at birth and grow rapidly, quadrupling their size within a fortnight, when they begin to emerge from the nest and learn to fend for themselves. They are fed by their mother for up to three weeks, but she may evict them when her next brood is born, by which time they are about half their adult size.

Some of the earliest young may be capable of breeding before the summer is out, so water voles have the capacity to produce large numbers of offspring in a year. However, their chances of surviving beyond six months are slim. As well as predators such as mink, water voles are in danger from owls and cats when moving to new territories. They suffer a high mortality rate at this time. Those born early in the season are likely to live longer than young born later on, and in rare cases may survive to see a third summer.

In winter, females with some of their offspring, and occasionally a few unrelated males, may nest communally. In early spring, high population densities can occur in some places and 20 or more voles may congregate in less than half a kilometre (quarter of a mile) of river bank. As spring progresses, they begin to spread out and by May all the breeding females have an exclusive territory, which they defend against intruders. Each territory occupies about 75–130m (250–430ft) of water's edge, with the males having larger ranges that may overlap the territories of several females.

During the breeding season, scent glands on the flanks become very enlarged and the animals scratch these with their hind feet. The males stomp their feet on the ground to mark it – a practice known as 'drum-marking' – and both sexes leave scent along their trails. This probably aids social recognition as well as marking territorial boundaries. On meeting, water voles may lash their tails

Although it is a good swimmer, the water vole does not have webbed feet.

Once at the surface, the water vole adopts a 'doggie paddle' swimming style, holding its nose well up out of the water. As the vole's eyes and ears are near the top of its head, it can see and hear without having to expose too much of itself above the surface.

and chatter their teeth. If a fight develops, they will grapple and bite each other, rolling over and over, sometimes causing serious wounds.

Signs of life

The activities of water voles are fairly conspicuous. Where they emerge from the water there may be a smooth wet patch, often forming a platform and sometimes with distinctive star-shaped prints – four toed from the forefeet and five toed from the hind feet. Droppings are oval, around 1cm (⅓in) long and

▼ Roots and bark are not the water vole's favourite food. However, in winter, supplies of fresh vegetation dwindle and the voles are forced to look for other sources of food.

UNDERGROUND NETWORK

Water vole burrow systems can be surprisingly complex, often having a number of chambers linked by a system of tunnels. When young are in the burrow, the parent vole may loosely seal the entrance with a wad of grass and perhaps also mud.

Entrances at water level are always in danger of flooding, and when the water table is particularly high the voles may not bother with a burrow at all. In such circumstances, they may build a nest above ground, in dense tussocks of grass or sedge. Seasonal flooding or bad weather has been known to drive water voles from their preferred waterside habitat. Away from water, they build more extensive burrow systems and live almost completely below ground.

▲ Normally there is at least one entrance to the burrow at or below the surface of the water. This enables the vole to enter and leave its home without having to come out into the open.

◄ Water vole prints in the soft mud at the side of a pond or river show the four distinct toes of the forefeet.

greenish brown or black, depending on what the voles have been eating and how long ago they were deposited. The droppings tend to be left in small heaps – or latrines – near where the animals leave the water, and help to delineate territory.

Water voles can be seen by day sitting up like squirrels and nibbling food held in their paws. They eat mainly grasses, sedges, reeds, rushes and other waterside plants, and consume nearly 80 per cent of their own body weight each day. Uneaten remains are left in small heaps. Piles of sedge leaves or reed stems with the juicy parts missing are typical water vole leftovers. They gnaw the base of tall plants to bring them down, as a forester might fell a tree. The best parts are eaten and the rest abandoned.

Sometimes voles move away from the water's edge to graze grass or eat crops, leaving bald patches as evidence. Where water voles live in high densities, they may consume up to a fifth of all the plant growth in the area. In autumn and winter, when many plants are dead or dormant, voles often turn to eating fallen fruit, roots, bulbs and the bark of waterside trees, such as willow and alder.

Species at risk

Water voles are prolific breeders and should not be threatened with dying out in Britain, yet there are disturbing signs that this is exactly what is happening.

The first National Water Vole survey, conducted in 1989–90, revealed that although the animal was still widespread, there seemed to be fewer numbers at each site than before and they appeared to have vanished altogether from about 70 per cent of places where they were known to have been present in the past. Even the otter's decline was not as dramatic. Worse still, a follow-up survey showed that the rate of decline had increased to about 90 per cent by 2000. Yet until recently this catastrophic state of affairs had scarcely been noticed.

Unless the causes of decline are understood, it is difficult to carry out effective practical measures to stop water voles from dying out in Britain. Pollution is a possible culprit, although voles are almost entirely vegetarian and are therefore unlikely to be affected by insecticides and poisons that accumulate in prey. Disease is another possibility, but there is no evidence that water voles have been affected by any specific diseases. Neither have winters been so severe as to cause problems for semi-aquatic

WATER VOLE OR WATER RAT?

Despite its country name of water rat, this enchanting animal is not a rat. The common brown rat, *Rattus norvegicus,* may be seen in similar waterside habitats, but there are several notable differences to help identify them.

Water voles have dark chestnut brown silky fur, with long glossy guard hairs projecting from the main coat, whereas the common rat has coarse, grey-brown, rather shaggy fur and looks dull rather than glossy. The vole's face is chubby and rounded, with small hairy ears; the rat has a pointed nose and more prominent fleshy ears.

The vole's tail is thin and looks dark (because it is hairy) and extends for about half the length of the body. A rat's tail is long – about three-quarters of its

▲ The rounded appearance and glossy fur is typical of water voles. In animals that are running, or stretching out, look for a thin, dark, hairy tail and tiny ears.

body length – scaly and naked, so it looks pinkish grey.

Voles are almost always seen in the water or at the water's edge, and are predominantly country animals. Rats are widely found in and around human habitations. When frightened, the vole dives from the bank with a 'plop', whereas rats slip silently into the water or dive in with a splash.

◀ A brown rat has noticeable ears and a pointed nose and face. The tail is longer and thicker than a water vole's and appears scaly.

creatures. River engineering works have certainly destroyed much of its valuable habitat, but the vole should have been safe in small streams and ponds.

The most frequently cited culprit is the American mink. Originally introduced to British fur farms, from the 1950s onwards the animals began escaping, resulting in a steady build-up of numbers in the wild. Mink eat water voles, which share the same habitat and are often too slow both on land and in water to escape this lithe

and amphibious predator. Once mink reach an area, water voles tend to vanish within a year or two. This observation led to the assumption that, since mink cannot easily be eradicated, the water vole was doomed to die out. However, this forecast overlooks the fact that the water vole's decline has been going on for decades and began long before mink became widely established. The problem is more complex than predatory mink alone.

Shrinking habitat

Research suggests that several interacting factors have probably contributed to the water vole's decline. The population is not spread evenly across the countryside. Instead, voles live on strips of land by the water's edge and if those strips are cut into short sections – by lining a river bank with concrete, for instance, or building along it – the vole population becomes fragmented. Each of these small colonies is vulnerable to chance events such as

Voles particularly like to feed on platforms of floating vegetation at the water's edge. They nibble through the bases of reeds to bring them down, eat the juicy parts and leave a litter of discarded fragments.

Creatures of habit

Water voles consistently use the same route to enter and leave the water. Smooth platforms develop on the banks of the river where the vegetation is trampled or worn away.

poor breeding (possibly brought on by stress, which causes females to produce male offspring only), floods drowning animals in their burrows, or physical damage to river banks by dredging machinery. Gaps between surviving groups widen and local vole populations become even more isolated and vulnerable. Mink arriving in such a pocket are quite likely to wipe out any remaining water voles.

In the past, water voles could have retreated into wet marshland but most such areas, especially beside lowland rivers (the best water vole habitat), have been drained to grow crops or provide better pasture. As a result, the water vole is restricted to a narrow band at the water's edge. Only here does the full range of plants on which it feeds continue to grow, but in this narrow strip there is nowhere to escape from prowling mink.

In good years, the breeding season can extend from March into October, which gives a healthy female time to raise as many as four litters. As soon the young are weaned, the female is ready to breed again.

Water voles need a variety of vegetation to survive, especially in winter when many plants die back or the water freezes, preventing access to underwater plants. Waterside plants are naturally very diverse, but if they are dredged out to improve water flow, or pollutants reduce the numbers of plant species, water voles find it increasingly hard to survive. Pollutants devastate plant life in two ways – either by killing the plants directly or doing so indirectly through a process called eutrophication (overfeeding), when a build-up of nitrates encourages a heavy surface growth of algae – known as a 'bloom' – that stops water plants growing.

These problems are less severe in reedbeds and marshland. Not only are there plenty of plants to eat all year round, but the dense reed stalks give water voles an escape route from mink. Perhaps the real problem for the water vole has been that this sort of refuge no longer exists in many lowland areas, leaving voles more vulnerable to predators. Now that the problems are better understood, however, it may be possible to try out various forms of habitat management so as to reduce the water vole's vulnerability.

WILDLIFE WATCH

Where can I see water voles?

● Water voles are naturally shy and more often heard than seen, as they scuffle in the vegetation and plop into the water. Find a place where there are signs of water vole activity, then sit and wait quietly. Search slow rivers and reedy ponds, and choose a mild day as water voles tend not to come out in extremes of heat or cold.

● Water vole tracks can be seen in the smooth mud where they enter and leave the water. Look for runs and tunnels in dense waterside vegetation. Feeding signs include small patches of cropped grasses, sedges and reeds, with little piles of discarded vegetable matter.

● Tame water voles can often be seen in the duck pens at Wildfowl and Wetland Trust sites, such as Slimbridge, Martin Mere and the London Wetland Centre in Barnes, south-west London. There is also a healthy population in the Norfolk Broads. Surprisingly, an increasingly good place to see water voles is in cities and towns located on rivers where the species has been encouraged or reintroduced.

The great crested grebe

Virtually wiped out in the 19th century, the elegant great crested grebe is once again a familiar diving bird, fascinating to watch as it hunts for fish and performs elaborate courtship displays.

Even in its relatively discreet, largely grey-brown autumn and winter plumage, the great crested grebe is a strikingly elegant bird. It swims with its streamlined, short-tailed body slung low in the water, and often holds its long white neck erect above its gleaming white breast. The grebe's white face and neat black cap frame a red eye, and a black eyestripe leads to a long, sharp bill.

The great crested could be mistaken for a red-necked grebe in winter plumage, or perhaps a red-throated diver, but its elegance gives it away. In its element, the great crested grebe is a supremely graceful bird, slipping swiftly through the water and often diving from sight in pursuit of fish and other prey. However, on land it is a different story, since – as with many specialised water birds – its legs are placed so far back on its body it can barely walk. This makes it extremely ungainly and vulnerable on land, and it normally avoids coming ashore.

Great crested grebes rarely take to the air, although they can fly quite fast on whirring wings, long necks slightly drooped and legs trailing behind. They are capable of fairly long migration flights from northern and eastern Europe. Heavy birds, they need a long take-off run to get airborne, pattering their feet over the water's surface like a swan as they go.

Autumn migration

The great crested grebe is the largest of the European grebes and the most widespread large grebe in Britain. Its regular summer breeding range extends as far north as the central lowlands of Scotland and the northern counties of Ireland, but in autumn these northern breeders move to regions where the water is less likely to freeze over. Many fly south to spend the winter months on lowland

The great crested grebe feeds on the open water of lakes, reservoirs and flooded gravel pits but it prefers them to be fringed with vegetation for cover and nesting.

lakes and reservoirs in the Midlands and southern England, while others head for sheltered coastal bays and quiet estuaries. In Northern Ireland, for example, roughly half of the 4000 or more grebes that breed on Lough Neagh migrate to the coastal waters of Belfast Lough in early autumn and in Scotland similar numbers gather on the Firth of Forth. They are joined by grebes that have flown south and west to escape freezing conditions in Europe, and in cold seasons these may outnumber the resident birds.

SPINY FOOD

Any waters occupied by great crested grebes must hold good stocks of their fish prey. The birds also take aquatic insects and molluscs, especially for their young. All these animals contain relatively indigestible parts such as shells, spines and bones. Like many other birds, grebes deal with this material by regurgitating it in pellets.

Adult grebes often swallow feathers, which they sometimes pluck from their own bodies. It is likely that this aids pellet formation and forms a cushion that stops fish bones piercing the bird's stomach. It also prolongs the digestion process, enabling some of the sharp material to be broken down. Parent birds regularly feed feathers to their young, even when they are less than a day old.

GREAT CRESTED GREBE FACT FILE

Adapted for life on and under the water, the great crested grebe moves awkwardly on land. It gathers in flocks on large lakes, estuaries and the sea in autumn, but breeds in pairs or loose colonies, displaying its breeding plumage to dramatic effect during courtship.

● NAMES
Common name: great crested grebe
Scientific name: *Podiceps cristatus*

● HABITAT
Lakes, reservoirs, gravel pits and slow-flowing rivers in breeding season; large lakes and reservoirs, rivers, estuaries and sea in winter

● DISTRIBUTION
Lowland England, Wales, southern Scotland and Ireland

● STATUS
More than 12,000 adults in summer; numbers swelled by continental immigrants in winter

● SIZE
Length 46–51cm (18–20in);
weight 750–1250g (1lb 10oz–2lb 12oz)

● KEY FEATURES
Dagger-like bill, long, slender, white-fronted neck, upperparts grey-brown, underparts white; breeding adult has pink bill, black crest, chestnut and black 'ruff' of tippets; non-breeding adult and juvenile have dark crown, white face, neck and chest, and lack tippets and full crest

● HABITS
Spends much time on water; frequently dives for fish; rarely seen in flight, which is usually low over water, with legs trailing behind

● VOICE
A range of mainly harsh, nasal, growling, crooning or clicking calls, which carry far across water

● FOOD
Mainly fish; aquatic insects and their larvae and other invertebrates fed to young

● BREEDING
February–September but mostly mid-April–mid-June; often has 2 broods

● NEST
Mound of soggy vegetation collected by both male and female; free-floating, anchored to vegetation or built up from bottom of water

● EGGS
Dull chalky white at first, staining orange-buff to dark brown as incubation progresses; usually 3–5 eggs (2 or 6 rare) laid at 2-day intervals; incubation begins with first egg, lasts 27–29 days per egg; hatching staggered

● YOUNG
Stripy blackish and pale buff head, neck and upperparts, red face, white breast and belly; ride on parents' backs for 3 weeks; fledge at 10–15 weeks; juveniles retain stripes on head and neck

Grebes have heavily lobed toes for propulsion through the water, instead of webbed feet like ducks and divers. They do not use their wings underwater like some other diving birds.

A black crest is prominent in the breeding season.
Both sexes have a white face and sharp bill.
Chestnut tippets are fringed with black.
Upperparts are greyish brown.
The neck is long, white and slender.
Underparts are white.

Distribution map key

Present all year round
Present during summer months
Spring and autumn passage migrant
Not present

Head-shaking display

This display occurs spontaneously when a pair of grebes is reunited after being apart. It may also be used to reinforce the pair bond after a territorial dispute with other grebes. When one pair begins this head-shaking display, other birds nearby will follow suit to strengthen their own pair bonds.

During the spectacular courtship dance the birds rise from the water breast to breast, holding weed in their bills. The display is performed only by pairs established on their territory, as a prelude to nest-building.

The pair waggle their heads, with crests and tippets held erect, sometimes giving clicking calls.

During intense periods of head shaking, one or both birds may flick up its feathers with its bill.

Silent head waggling continues with the bill held raised and closed, and the tippets partly flattened. This activity is interspersed with slower head turns.

As the grebes display they slowly drift apart, maintaining an erect posture and giving twanging calls.

The early migrants moult into winter plumage after arrival. Like ducks, grebes moult their feathers within a short period, during which they cannot fly. This makes them vulnerable to attack, so they roost on the water, often in 'rafts' of a hundred or so. From September they are joined by grebes that moult before migrating, and so arrive in their winter plumage.

Taking the plunge

Although great crested grebes gather to roost, they normally hunt alone. They feed mainly on small fish, plus other animals such as shrimps and aquatic insects, catching them underwater by diving beneath the surface. Before diving, a grebe will make itself less buoyant, expelling the air in its plumage by drawing its feathers closer to its body. This is a way of telling when a grebe is about to dive.

To keep its feathers waterproof and in good order, a grebe preens regularly and often, using its bill to collect oil from the preen gland at the base of its tail and apply it to its plumage. To ensure that breast and belly feathers are well coated, the bird turns on its side in the water, revealing its gleaming white underparts.

DID YOU KNOW?

By the 1860s great crested grebes had been hunted to the edge of extinction in Britain. They were killed for their feathers, which were used on hats and other accessories. Their plight helped to inspire bird-lovers of the day to form societies opposed to the killing of birds for their feathers. These organisations combined to form the Society for the Protection of Birds in 1889. In 1904 it gained royal patronage and has since gone from strength to strength as the RSPB.

GREAT CRESTED GREBE CALENDAR

JANUARY • FEBRUARY

Most individuals spend the winter on estuaries and shallower regions of the sea. Some overwinter on rivers close to their breeding lakes, and pair formation and display often occurs at this time.

MARCH • APRIL

By spring, the adults have returned to their breeding haunts. Pairs continue to display and begin to build their nests, which are substantial floating rafts of aquatic vegetation.

MAY • JUNE

With nest building complete, a clutch of up to six chalky white eggs is laid. The stripy young have generally hatched by May. When small, the young ride on their parents' backs for protection.

JULY • AUGUST

The parent birds divide the brood and care for several chicks each. The adults continue to feed the youngsters for at least 10 weeks, but they are increasingly able to find their own food.

SEPTEMBER • OCTOBER

Both adults and juveniles begin to disperse from their breeding territories in autumn, forming flocks on larger lakes and rivers. Eventually, these birds may move to estuaries and the sea.

NOVEMBER • DECEMBER

Established on their wintering grounds, grebes usually feed alone, but form loose flocks when resting. Birds on inland lakes may have problems if ice forms. Some birds start forming pairs.

After preening, the grebe often rises out of the water and shakes, sending a shower of water flying in all directions.

Breeding finery

Before the birds leave their wintering grounds to return to their breeding territories, both sexes discard their dark grey-brown and white winter plumage and begin to develop their splendid breeding attire. This consists of fine blackish, erectile, double crests on the tops of their heads and dark orange plumes, called 'tippets', fringed with black, on their cheeks. The effect is dramatic, part of their pre-nesting displays.

Great crested grebes move back to their breeding waters from mid-February onwards, depending on the weather and ice cover. They favour shallow lowland waters such as small freshwater lakes, reservoirs, flooded gravel pits and large rivers, with plentiful prey and a good growth of marginal vegetation to conceal

their nests. In the south, some birds are able to stay on their breeding territories throughout the year and their courtship displays can be seen as early as December. Birds forced away from their breeding grounds by freezing weather conditions generally delay their displays until they return in spring. Then they gather in loose flocks, pair up and start to dance.

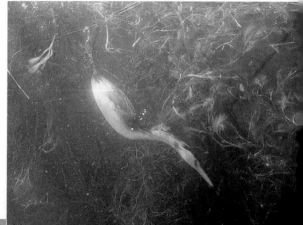

▶ As the grebe dives in search of a meal, it drives itself through the water using its yellowy green lobed feet. Its legs are positioned well back on its body for maximum power and manoeuvrability.

The grebe feeds mainly on fish, which it chases underwater at a depth of around 2–4m (6–13ft). It can stay submerged for 30 seconds or more, but despite the bird's hunting skill, its prey sometimes escapes.

EXTENDED FAMILY

The great crested grebe is one of five grebe species that either breed in Britain, or are autumn and winter visitors.

The little grebe is the smallest species, as well as the most widespread. As with the other grebes, its plumage varies from season to season. During the autumn and winter, its pale buff cheeks, neck and underside contrast with a dark brown cap, back and wings, and it has a conspicuous whitish 'powder puff' tail end. During the breeding season it is generally darker, with chestnut cheeks and throat, and a creamy coloured patch at the base of its short bill.

Little grebes are heard more frequently than seen. Their far-carrying, whinnying calls, which are sometimes given as a duet, often echo around their territories, while the birds stay hidden. However, once their presence is established, a little patience is usually rewarded with a good view. During the breeding season the birds are fiercely territorial and there are frequent disputes between neighbouring pairs. In winter they relax and form small groups, usually on more open fresh waters, but they move to the coast in especially cold periods.

The handsome Slavonian grebe is a rare breeding species in Britain, with fewer than 70 pairs nesting in the Scottish Highlands each year. The RSPB reserve at Loch Ruthven near Inverness offers the best opportunities to see them in breeding plumage, but they should not be sought out elsewhere as they are protected during the nesting season. In autumn and winter however, the species occurs around coasts, on estuaries and occasionally inland. At this time it has a dark back, hind-neck and cap down to eye level, with contrasting white cheeks and white neck front.

Another rare breeder is the black-necked grebe, with a breeding population that fluctuates between 40 and 80 pairs each year. Most breed in the Scottish Highlands, but there is sporadic nesting activity elsewhere. In autumn, winter migrants from eastern Europe may be seen on lakes, with a few on sheltered coasts and estuaries. They resemble Slavonian grebes but with steeper, higher foreheads, a dark cap extending below the eyes and dusky cheeks with the white of the throat extending into a vertical crescent at the rear.

The red-necked grebe is a scarce winter visitor, occurring mainly on east coast estuaries, although occasionally seen on inland waters. Its black cap fades into pale cheeks, brightened by a yellow base to the beak. It sometimes lingers into early summer, when it develops the chestnut-red neck from which it derives its name.

▲ Also known as the dabchick, the little grebe is very secretive during the breeding season, when it favours still or slow-flowing waters with emergent or overhanging vegetation.

▲ The red-necked grebe arrives in small numbers in October and leaves in March. During this time it can be confused with the great crested grebe, but it is stockier and has a shorter, thicker, greyer neck.

◀ The Slavonian grebe breeds in very small numbers on shallow freshwater lochs in Scotland. In breeding plumage it has golden ear tufts, a contrasting black head, chestnut flanks and a dark back.

▲ One distinguishing feature of the black-necked grebe, which from autumn may sometimes be seen in the company of Slavonian grebes, is the slimmer, slightly upswept bill.

Ceremonial displays

The elaborate courtship displays of great crested grebes can be divided into phases, each with its own set of movements. The discovery ceremony is performed when the birds are first pairing up, before they establish a breeding territory. It often begins when one of the pair dives just below the surface, creating a bow wave. Meanwhile the other bird holds its wings out to the side and its head low in a position referred to as the 'cat posture'. The swimming bird surfaces in an upright 'penguin posture', with its beak held low, then rotates to face its partner.

The grebes then display their crests and tippets to each other by repeated head shaking. As they dance, they slowly drift apart before diving and surfacing with weed in their beaks. They swim towards each other, and when they meet they rise vertically from the water and

The brood of chicks often rides on one parent's back, in the shelter of its wings, while the other adult goes off to hunt. A parent returning with food is always greeted with shrill squeaks of excitement from its ever-hungry offspring.

Great crested grebes take turns to incubate their eggs, although the female sits for longer than the male. When a bird returns from fishing, it often sits on the nest with its wings outspread to dry.

dance breast to breast, their feet frantically treading water. They swing the weed from side to side before subsiding.

In the retreat ceremony, which often occurs after the pair have had an encounter with intruders or rivals, one bird takes a ceremonial flight past the other. It patters across the water, suddenly stops and adopts the cat posture. The pair may then link up and indulge in some mutual head shaking.

Floating nest

Once they are fully established on their territory, the pair start to build their nest. This is a heap of floating vegetation, collected over several days and anchored to growing plants to stop it drifting away. Once it has sufficient mass and buoyancy, the female starts laying her eggs, usually between three and five at two-day intervals. Both birds incubate them until the chicks hatch some four weeks later. Throughout the nesting period the birds add more vegetation to their floating nursery. This is vital, as it is constantly decomposing and without extra material it would disappear.

When the chicks hatch, they look quite unlike their parents. They are fluffy and striped along their heads, necks and bodies from head to tail, for camouflage among waterside vegetation. The chicks are capable of swimming unaided immediately after hatching but at this stage could easily be taken by their main enemy, the pike. To avoid this risk, the

young grebes often ride on their parents' backs, hidden between the parent birds' folded wings.

Once all the eggs have hatched, the nest is abandoned. The full brood rides on one parent's back while the other adult collects food such as small insects and later fish. When the chicks are two to three weeks old they spend less time being ferried around and swim more, although they often stay hidden among

The water courtship of the great crested grebe consists of ritualised ceremonial displays. These can be divided into four sections, each containing different stylised movements, which both birds perform.

vegetation. This enables both parents to collect food for the entire brood. The chicks rely on their parents for food until they are 10 to 15 weeks old, although they begin trying to catch their own long before this. By the time summer gives way to autumn the young birds are able to fly and can accompany the adults as they leave for their winter quarters.

Where can I see great crested grebes?

● In autumn many great crested grebes move to the coast, but many more are to be seen on lakes, reservoirs and gravel pits. In spring and summer, canals and large, slow-flowing rivers in southern England are good places to look. The Norfolk Broads provide plenty of opportunities to watch both great crested and little grebes.

● Rutland Water and Grafham Water support numerous grebes, especially in autumn and winter. These huge expanses of water rarely freeze over, so there are usually birds present all year round. A telescope is helpful to identify the birds from a distance.

● Dungeness RSPB reserve in Kent is a good site for wintering grebes, including the great crested. If the gravel pits are frozen over, look at the sea. Check the flocks carefully, as red-necked grebes are sometimes present.

● Lough Neagh and nearby lakes in Northern Ireland form the main breeding stronghold of great crested grebes in Britain. This is one of the premier sites in the whole range of the species, which extends throughout much of Europe and Asia.

Coots and moorhens

Out on the open water of rivers and ponds, gregarious coots dive to scavenge food from submerged vegetation, while the more nervous moorhen swims warily among the plants on the water's edge.

Both the coot and the moorhen belong to the family of birds called rails, which are generally very shy and difficult to see. However, in Britain at least, both are usually fairly bold or even tame, allowing close observation.

The coot is larger and plumper than the moorhen and is further distinguished by its white bill and by the white 'frontal shield' of horny skin on its forehead. The moorhen has a striking red frontal shield, a red bill with a yellow tip and a white inverted 'V' shape on its tail, which it frequently flicks. When swimming, the moorhen holds its tail almost as high as its head.

Both coots and moorhens feed mainly on water plants, insects and tadpoles, but will also venture into surrounding fields to find snails and earthworms. Coots tend

▶ Male and female moorhens take equal responsibility for feeding and protecting their offspring. The young will be entirely dependent on their parents for food until they are about a month old.

Moorhen tail-flick display

The tail-flick display is typical moorhen behaviour. Modified forms of the action are used in courtship, territorial disputes and to lay claim to food.

▲ The characteristic white patch of bare skin on the coot's forehead explains the origins of the phrase 'as bald as a coot'.

The moorhen's swimming action involves much head bobbing...

...and a slight flicking of the tail as it makes progress using its large, unwebbed feet.

to congregate in loose flocks to dive for food in dense beds of submerged vegetation. Their bodies are very buoyant, so in order to dive they must flatten their feathers, expelling any air trapped in their plumage. When they dive, they jump forward and downward, bobbing back up to the surface in the same spot a few seconds later.

While underwater, coots may catch small fish or leeches, as well as tadpoles, but most often they pluck vigorously at the underwater vegetation, dragging pieces of plant back up to the surface to eat. This activity is sometimes interrupted by another hungry coot, or by black-headed gulls that gather on the surface waiting for the chance to steal a snack.

Breeding habits

Both coots and moorhens build cup-shaped nests among aquatic vegetation, often raised above the water level with a ramp leading down. Moorhens lay five to eight eggs, but their nests often contain more than this because one female may simply lay her eggs in the nest of another and then abandon them. The advantage of this 'egg dumping' is that the offspring will be reared by a responsible mother. Birds nesting close together are likely to be related to each other, and both coots and moorhens are quite likely to adopt – or even kidnap – young birds from another brood.

If conditions are good, coots will have two broods a year, laying five to nine eggs each time, and moorhens will have two or three broods. Often young from the first brood of the season can be seen helping to rear their siblings from later broods. This may simply entail feeding and protecting them, but sometimes it even extends to incubation and brooding.

COOT AND MOORHEN CALENDAR

JANUARY • FEBRUARY

Cold weather is bad for coots and moorhens if their homes become frozen. Their search for open water often leads them to overwinter in brackish estuaries or near power stations where the water is warmer.

MARCH • JUNE

In March, coots lay their first clutches. Moorhens begin to nest in April and the chicks hatch throughout May and June, looking like dark balls of fluff with red foreheads and blue crowns.

JULY • AUGUST

The breeding season continues with second and replacement clutches. Fully grown young from earlier nests, now able to look after themselves, may be seen caring for newly hatched siblings.

SEPTEMBER • DECEMBER

As the last broods mature and adults complete their full moult, some birds, especially young ones, move away to form small flocks. They are often joined by migrants from eastern and northern Europe.

In case of danger from predators, both coots and moorhens frequently adopt the survival strategy of splitting the brood between the parents. In both species, the female usually continues to use the nest as her base, while the male builds a special brooding platform, without a nest cup, for his troop of chicks. If one of these platforms has to be constructed for the first brood, it may later be upgraded into a main nest for the second or a later nesting attempt.

The white 'flags' at each side under the tail are used in ritualised display movements to demonstrate a claim to territory.

The bird dips its head with each swimming stroke...

...then momentarily flicks its tail flags into the air.

MOORHEN FACT FILE

A pigeon-sized waterbird, the moorhen may be seen on most expanses of freshwater in Britain, its head nodding forward as it swims. When extremely alarmed it will dive and remain submerged with just its bill visible above water.

● NAMES
Common name: moorhen, common moorhen
Scientific name: *Gallinula chloropus*

● HABITAT
Ponds, lakes, rivers, streams, water-filled ditches

● DISTRIBUTION
All over the British Isles except in most mountainous areas

● STATUS
About 240,000 territories in England and 75,000 in Ireland

● SIZE
Length 32–35cm (13–14in); weight 250–420g (9–15oz)

● KEY FEATURES
Slim and nervous; dark blue-grey and olive-brown, looks black at a distance; adult has distinctive bright red frontal shield, yellow tip to the bright red bill and red eyes; distinctive ragged white streak along flanks; rear has inverted 'V' of white feathers on the undertail; tail constantly flicks

● HABITS
Grazes water plants, leaves from trees and bushes, and grass

● VOICE
Typical call is an explosive 'pwark' or 'kittick' – loud and urgent if alarmed, softer when used as contact call; gives varied rhythmic calls on night flights (often mistaken for an owl)

● FOOD
Vegetable matter, molluscs, insects, earthworms, sometimes small fish, tadpoles and occasionally birds' eggs

● BREEDING
April–September; family parties with large young still being fed can be seen into early October

● NEST
Usually in vegetation growing in the water, even floating; sometimes on solid ground, in low bushes or in trees; high nests may be based on remains of another bird's nest or even a squirrel's drey; nest is a neat platform of twigs and stems with a deep grass cup to hold eggs

● EGGS
Smooth and glossy, off-white or pale buff with dark blotches often concentrated at blunt end; clutches of 5–8 eggs; old birds lay more eggs than young ones, largest clutches laid mid-season; incubation about 3 weeks; 2, sometimes 3, broods a year; 2 females, sometimes 3, can lay in the same nest

● YOUNG
Scrawny, dark fluffy chicks, with bare blue crown and red forehead; leave nest immediately; often brooded in first 2 weeks, especially in cold or wet weather; parents and young from earlier broods feed chicks for up to 40–50 days, until they can fly

Distribution map key

■ Present

□ Not present

The red horny frontal shield and red and yellow bill are distinctive features of adults but not juvenile birds.

The moorhen reveals its white undertail coverts in a frequent tail-flicking display.

Red garters occur at the top of the legs.

Plumage is very dark blue-grey, almost black, and dark olive-brown relieved by a distinctive ragged row of white feathers on the flank.

The yellow-green legs appear disproportionately long and the feet are enormous.

Specially adapted feet
The lobed toes of the coot and the long toes of the moorhen may appear to be poor substitutes for the webbed feet of most waterfowl, but both birds' feet are perfectly suited to their needs. The coot's lobed toes work well for swimming, closing as the foot comes forwards, to offer least resistance to the water, and opening as it pushes backwards, to propel the bird onwards. The unwebbed separate toes enable the coot to grasp hold of tangled reeds and vegetation.

The moorhens' long toes enable them to walk on land without difficulty. They sometimes even climb and nest in trees.

Moorhen territories can be small with as little as 8m (26ft) between nests. Nonetheless, these are vigorously defended, especially during the breeding season.

As a coot dives, the air trapped in its plumage is squeezed out in a stream of bubbles. These can give away the bird's position to scavengers hoping to steal food from the coot when it surfaces.

Another important advantage for both birds is being able to walk on floating vegetation. The long toes and spreading feet allow the birds to distribute their weight so that they do not sink.

Their large feet also enable the birds to run across the water, which they have to do in order to take off. The resulting weak and laboured flight, with long legs and big feet trailing well behind the tail, does not take the birds very far and hardly seems worth the effort of the long pattering run.

Many predators

Neither coots nor moorhens are long-lived birds, as they are threatened by a variety of predators at every stage in their life cycle. Their nests are easy to see and eggs are lost to all sorts of animals. Brown rats are good swimmers and often frequent the edges of freshwater, taking advantage of any vulnerable eggs or baby birds they come across. Grass snakes love water and most adults are able to tackle a moorhen egg, although coots' eggs may be too big for some individuals. Crows and magpies also steal eggs.

Once hatched, the chicks are in danger from predators both above and below the water. Predatory fish, including pike, may snatch the swimming chicks from below, while birds of prey, such as marsh harriers and kestrels, occasionally swoop down to seize unwary juveniles.

COOT FACT FILE

Larger and bolder than the moorhen, the coot is a rotund waterbird. When it does venture on to land to feed, which it may do in autumn and winter, it prefers to be in the open away from cover, unlike moorhens.

● **NAMES**
Common names: coot, common coot, Eurasian coot
Scientific name: *Fulica atra*

● **HABITAT**
Ponds, lakes, rivers, streams, flooded gravel pits, estuaries and even sea in prolonged freezing weather in winter

● **DISTRIBUTION**
Throughout the British Isles, apart from north-west Scotland and the mountains of western England and Wales

● **STATUS**
About 46,000 adults in Britain and 9000 in Ireland

● **SIZE**
Length 36–38cm (14–15in); weight 575–900g (20–32oz)

● **KEY FEATURES**
Dark, duck-shaped with a pointed white bill and white frontal shield; round, red eyes; greenish legs; wings have pale trailing edges

● **HABITS**
Up-ends and regularly dives for food in water up to 2m (6ft 6in) deep, occasionally even 5m (16ft 6in) deep; will steal food from other coots; grazes grass on land near water

● **VOICE**
Harsh, loud 'kwok', 'kuke' and 'kt-twok'; also explosive, abrupt 'ptik' that sounds like metal on stone

● **FOOD**
Largely vegetable matter; also small fish, snails, leeches, insects and tadpoles

● **BREEDING**
First clutches may be laid in late March; replacement and second clutches produced until end of July

● **NEST**
A bulky structure made from plant material heaped together in vegetation growing in up to 30cm (12in) of water; added to if water level rises; eggs laid in grass-lined cup

● **EGGS**
Bigger and much less blotchy than those of the moorhen; glossy and off-white with even speckling; clutch size mostly 5–9; incubation starts before the clutch is complete and lasts just over 3 weeks; eggs hatch over several days

● **YOUNG**
Feed themselves at about 4 weeks and begin to fly at about 8 weeks

Distribution map key

■ Present during summer

□ Not present

The legs are long, and the toes have pronounced lobes to aid swimming.

The body plumage is dark with no white markings.

The white bill sometimes has a pinkish tinge. The distinctive bald forehead makes the bird easy to recognise from a distance.

OTHER RAILS AND CRAKES

The water rail (*Rallus aquaticus*) is less common than coots and moorhens, but it is still quite numerous in reedbeds and among damp vegetation in many parts of Britain. It has a fairly long red bill, dark-striped brown back, black and white bars on the flanks and bluish grey underparts. At about 25cm (10in) long it is smaller and slimmer than the moorhen, and very shy.

The best chance of seeing one is to find a nature reserve with a reedbed hide where the birds are used to coming out into the open areas between the reeds. In an extensive reedbed, trying to spot the water rails that are very likely to be living there is like looking for a needle in a huge haystack. However, their presence may be given away by the most amazing repertoire of cries and screams uttered by the birds. This habit, which occurs throughout the year, is well enough known to have its own country name – 'sharming' – and some of the sounds have been likened to the

▶ A water rail is daintier than the moorhen, with a longer beak and a very narrow body for slipping easily through reeds and other dense vegetation.

grunting and squealing of piglets. Often a pair will duet, with the male uttering slower, lower notes, answered by the female's higher and faster calls. Many of the birds present in the winter are visitors that have travelled west from central Europe.

In late summer and early autumn you may see the jet black chicks making their first forays through the reeds.

Water rails do a lot of climbing around in the reedbeds and eat all sorts of invertebrates, amphibians, fish and even small mammals and birds. Bigger prey items are killed by repeated blows to the back of the head. The bird uses its whole body like a hammer, rotating stiffly from the ankles.

◀ Traditional hay meadows are the preferred habitat of the corncrake. The bird tends to avoid pasture because of the threat of its nest being trampled.

Water rails are very fast and agile and have been seen to snatch small birds, such as wrens, in flight. Bird ringers have to be careful when catching birds in reedbeds where water rails live in case the birds caught in their nets are attacked.

Other, much rarer, members of the rail family found in Britain and Ireland are four species of crakes. The spotted crake (*Porzana porzana*) breeds sporadically in wet marshy sites. The birds are shy and difficult to see, but they have a characteristic whip-crack call that draws attention to their presence.

The corncrake (*Crex crex*), with a rasping call that sounds exactly like its scientific name, is another elusive species.

It used to be a common bird of hay meadows throughout the summer in the British Isles. Today it is restricted almost entirely to the far north and west where the hay crop is harvested late in the year. Elsewhere hay is harvested too early in the year for the birds to be able to complete their breeding cycle.

Corncrake-friendly hay-making, subsidised by conservationists, has stopped the decline in some areas. As well as late harvesting, this involves cutting the fields from the centre outwards so that the young birds can escape the blades of the cutters.

Tiny cousins of the spotted crake, the little crake and Baillon's crake, are rare wanderers from Europe sometimes seen in marshy areas.

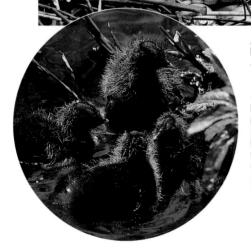

▲ Coots often have a second brood, which may be reared as late as early September.

◀ Downy coot chicks have bare red skin with a blue patch over the eye, as do moorhen chicks. They can be distinguished by the scraggy ruff of orange-red down on the sides of the head and neck, which is lacking in moorhen chicks.

Defending territory

Coots are by nature territorial and rather bad-tempered. They will sometimes charge at other waterfowl for no apparent reason, running head down at high speed. The same threatening display will be used to deter birds and animals considerably larger than themselves.

The coot runs and walks by placing each foot directly in front of the other. The size of the feet means the strides must be high and swinging, giving the bird an awkward, loping gait.

As the young grow, these hazards become less of a problem, but the birds then represent a bigger and better meal for larger predators. The greatest mammalian threat is the fox, which takes as many moorhens as otters and mink – all three species are probably capable of taking coots, too. Avian predators include the sparrowhawk – usually the bigger females – and the marsh harrier. These aerial hunters are expert at snatching waterbirds from the surface of lakes and rivers, and their lethal efficiency is illustrated by the panic and sudden crash-diving that breaks out among groups of coots whenever one flies over.

Food for poachers

In times past, moorhens and their eggs were one of the traditional foods for travellers. Since moorhens are difficult to pluck, they would be covered with clay and roasted in the embers of a fire in much the same way as hedgehogs were prepared. The birds were popular because they were easy to catch in snares and traps that would not alert the gamekeeper, who did not put any great value on them anyway. Coots were safe from poachers because they could not be caught without using a noisy firearm.

Ironically, coots were more at risk from landowners because they were seen as competition for the food resources they shared with more highly valued ducks. Before the official shooting season started, special shoots were organised that concentrated solely on coots. Today, however, both moorhens and coots enjoy somewhat safer lives although some are still shot under licence.

WILDLIFE WATCH

Where can I see coots and moorhens?

● These birds are found on most areas of water. They are closely related, but easy to tell apart. Coots, with their distinctive white frontal shields, are quite likely to be out on the open water in flocks, looking rotund and duck-like. Moorhens are likely to be at the edge of the water in the emergent vegetation, flicking their tails. Moorhen adults look dark blue-black when compared to the dark grey-black of the coots and coots' plumage lacks any white.

● Coots up-end in shallow water and frequently dive in order to find their food on the bottom or in the water weed. Like geese, they often graze grass on banks near the water.

● Moorhens take food items mainly along the water's margins, although they do sometimes graze grass and leaves from bushes. They seldom up-end or dive. Their most characteristic behaviour is the flicking of the tail to show the inverted 'V' of white under-tail coverts, and they also bob their heads when swimming.

● Coots are always associated with larger, open stretches of water, but moorhens will live happily on the smallest farm ponds and even in tiny ditches. The birds can often be seen walking across roads or on verges, feeding in places where there is no obvious waterway.

● Coots have benefited from the boom in the building industry because the quarrying of sand and gravel usually leaves behind flooded pits that provide an excellent habitat.

◄ Moorhens may build more than one nest in a season – sometimes a new one for each of three broods. Typically a clutch consists of 5–8 eggs, but a nest may contain up to 20 eggs, laid by more than one female.

The threat display is typical of many waterbirds, with the head down and neck stretched forwards.

The angry coot half-raises its wings, making it appear bigger and more intimidating to the creature it is trying to scare away.

Recognising geese

The sight of large formations of wild geese passing overhead – their long-necked bodies starkly silhouetted against the sky – is one of the most evocative images of autumn.

For thousands of years geese have been hunted for their feathers and their meat but now most of the important British and Irish wintering sites for migrant species have been designated official sanctuaries, and the birds tend to congregate there in flocks of varying sizes.

Most species of wild geese seen in Britain are visiting migrants that breed in higher latitudes and travel south to escape the cold winters of the Arctic and northern Europe. However, three species do nest in Britain – the greylag goose, the Canada goose and the Egyptian goose, which – despite its name – is in fact a duck. During autumn and winter greylag numbers are augmented by migrants from Iceland. The Canada goose and the Egyptian goose are not indigenous but have become established over the last three or four hundred years.

Family groups

All geese tend to pair for life and pairings are reinforced by complex, ritualised displays. Pairs of greylag and white-fronted geese, for example, perform a 'triumph ceremony' each time they meet that re-enacts their original courtship.

Geese are vigilant parents, guarding the nest and looking after their offspring for some time. Family ties last into the autumn and migrant birds usually arrive in family groups that stay together throughout the winter.

An essentially vegetarian diet means that geese are mostly associated with areas of grassland or other fairly short vegetation. Unlike their cousins the swans, which feed mostly while on water, they prefer to graze stubble fields and pastures. Their beaks are strong and serrated and make short work of scything through the plants. With the exception of the Egyptian goose, they are all vociferous. Their loud cackling, barking, yelping, growling, trumpeting or honking calls are often heard before the birds are seen as they fly low over the water to their roosting sites at dusk.

Bean geese are among the scarcest of the grey geese in Britain, confined to a handful of regularly visited wintering grounds. This species is wary and difficult to approach.

EASY GUIDE TO SPOTTING GEESE

Canada goose

Brent goose

Barnacle goose

Egyptian goose

Bean goose

Greylag goose

Pink-footed goose

White-fronted goose

WHAT ARE GEESE?

● Geese are wildfowl, members of the family Anatidae. Compared to their close relatives – the ducks – most species are large with characteristically long necks.

● Canada, Brent and barnacle geese all belong to the genus *Branta,* often referred to as 'black' geese.

● Greylag, pink-footed, bean and white-fronted geese all belong to the genus *Anser*, the so-called 'grey' geese.

● The Egyptian goose is misleadingly named, since it is more closely related to the shelduck than to geese. It belongs to the genus *Alopochen*.

HOW CAN I IDENTIFY GEESE?

● The colour will show whether a goose belongs to the black or grey group but identifying a particular species can be tricky.

● The Canada goose is the most widespread goose species in the British Isles. It can be recognised by its black head and neck, white chin and cheek strap, and grey-brown body plumage. Healthy Brent and barnacle geese never occur in the wild in summer. Brent geese appear essentially all dark except for the white stern and belly and the small white neck patch seen in adults. Barnacle geese look strikingly black and white from a distance.

● The four species of grey geese that commonly occur in the British Isles have similar

grey-brown plumage. However, the greylag goose has a large orange bill and pinkish legs; the pink-footed goose has a stubby dark bill with a pink band, pink legs and a short, brown neck. The bean goose has a dark bill with a variable patch of orange and orange legs, plus a very dark head and a long, dark neck.

The white-fronted goose has a pink or orange bill – depending on the sub-species – and orange legs. Variable amounts of dark barring are seen on the belly and the adult has a white forehead.

● The Egyptian goose has grey-brown plumage with a dark eye patch and collar. The bill and legs are pink and there are white patches on the forewings.

WILDLIFE WATCH

Where can I see geese?

● The best places to see wild geese are Wildfowl and Wetlands Trust (WWT) reserves. Well-placed hides enable visitors to see large numbers of birds at close range. Most reserves have extensive collections of wildfowl, including exotic as well as native species.

● The reserve at Slimbridge in Gloucester, headquarters of the WWT, is particularly good for winter-visiting white-fronted geese.

● Migrants visiting the north of Britain, such as barnacle geese, congregate at the WWT Caerlaverock reserve on the Solway Firth, near Dumfries (telephone 01387 770 200). The entire breeding population from

Svalbard winters there, as well as many pink-footed geese and greylags.

● In winter, thousands of pink-footed geese, plus a few wild barnacle and greylag geese, may be seen at WWT Martin Mere reserve on Merseyside.

● The WWT reserve at Arundel in West Sussex attracts large numbers of wild geese every winter.

● Well-populated Irish sites include Strangford Lough (NI), the Shannon estuary and Wexford Bay.

● Tame greylags, barnacle and Egyptian geese and wild Canada geese may often be seen in town parks with lakes.

Distribution map key

| | Present all year round | | Not present | | Present during winter months |

CANADA GOOSE *Branta canadensis*

Europe's largest goose is recognised by its black head and neck with large white face patch and contrasting brown plumage. Juveniles have duller plumage. The birds stay in family groups and are aggressive towards rivals.

● **SIZE**
Length 90–110cm (3–3½ft)

● **NEST**
Large pile of vegetation, near water or in reeds

● **BREEDING**
5–6 creamy white eggs laid in late March–May

● **FOOD**
Mainly aquatic plants, roots, shoots and seeds; bread and scraps from humans

● **HABITAT**
Lakes, parkland, gravel pits, meadows

● **VOICE**
Deep, far-carrying two-note calls; 'a-honk' rising on second syllable

● **DISTRIBUTION**
Established on farmland and in city parks with large lakes; some on sheltered estuaries

Black neck and head with white chin strap

Brown upperparts look barred

Introduced in the 17th century from North America, Canada geese are now common throughout much of Britain.

BRENT GOOSE *Branta bernicla*

A small bird, the brent goose appears very dark at a distance. In flight its striking white rump and tail show up clearly. Two distinct sub-species occur in the British Isles – one pale-bellied and one dark-bellied. The pale-bellied race breeds in Greenland and Svalbard and winters in Ireland, while the dark-bellied race, shown here, breeds in Russia and winters in eastern and southern Britain.

● **SIZE**
Length 55–60cm (22–24in)

● **BREEDING**
Does not breed in British Isles

● **FOOD**
Eelgrass in winter; algae and other saltmarsh plants

● **HABITAT**
Arctic tundra in summer, coastal marshes in winter

● **VOICE**
Deep, throaty 'rrronk' or 'kruk' call. Flocks produce a far-carrying growling or babbling sound

● **DISTRIBUTION**
Common winter visitor to quiet estuaries in eastern Britain and Ireland

Small black head and short neck with white collar

Back and wings are dark grey-brown, except for black flight feathers

Brilliant white rump and tail, especially noticeable in flight

Brent geese numbers fell in the 1930s when their main winter foodplant, eelgrass, was reduced by disease. Strict protection measures have aided their recovery and they are no longer rare.

BARNACLE GOOSE *Branta leucopsis*

Larger than the Brent goose, the barnacle goose has a black neck and white face, a grey-and-black barred back and white underparts. Juveniles have a mottled face and a more diffuse pattern of barring on the back. In flight, a conspicuous white 'V' shape can be seen on the black tail and rump.

Barnacle geese feed in large noisy flocks. They do not fly in regular formation.

● **SIZE**
Length 58–70cm (23–28in)

● **BREEDING**
Does not breed in the wild in British Isles

● **FOOD**
Plant material; especially leaves, stems and seeds

● **HABITAT**
Arctic tundra in summer; coastal marshes, estuaries and farmland in winter

● **VOICE**
High-pitched barking call

● **DISTRIBUTION**
Wild birds common in the north; feral birds widespread

Back barred black and grey

Black head, neck and breast with creamy face

BEAN GOOSE *Anser fabalis*

This large, mostly brown goose has a dark bill with a variable orange band near the tip, and its long legs and feet are noticeably bright orange. In flight, the wings and back look all dark above, apart from the paler tail with a very narrow terminal white band and narrow white base. A wary bird, the bean goose usually feeds in open fields where it can keep an eye open for danger and take flight easily.

The bean goose's head and neck are dark chocolate brown. This large goose is a scarce visitor from northern Scandinavia and Russia.

● **SIZE**
Length 65–80cm (2ft 2in–2ft 8in)

● **BREEDING**
Does not breed in British Isles

● **FOOD**
Grasses, grain and root crops

● **HABITAT**
Breeds on Arctic tundra and in open forests; overwinters on wet fields in southern Scotland and in Norfolk and Suffolk

● **VOICE**
Deep, loud cackling 'kayak'

● **DISTRIBUTION**
Winter visitor to Britain in small numbers

Robust bill, ideal for grazing grass

Sturdy, strong neck

Relatively long orange legs

Wide grey tail band

GREYLAG GOOSE *Anser anser*

A large, robust goose, the greylag has mostly grey plumage and an orange bill. The short, rounded tail is mostly white with a narrow grey 'V'. In flight, the pale grey forewings are noticeable. The sexes are alike and juveniles are similar to adults, but more barred on the upperparts and generally rather duller. Wild greylags are nervous birds and will take off noisily if threatened.

Within a flock of greylags, a few birds will scan the horizon for any sign of danger.

● **SIZE**
Length 75–90cm (2ft 6in–3ft)

● **NEST**
Hollow among tall vegetation

● **BREEDING**
4–6 creamy white eggs laid in April–May

● **FOOD**
Grasses, roots, cereals

● **HABITAT**
Marshy arable land, lake margins

● **VOICE**
Loud, deep cackling 'aang-ung-unk' call

● **DISTRIBUTION**
Winter visitor to northern Scotland; escapees/introductions found in other parts of British Isles

Large head and thick neck

Back feathers have pale margins

Legs pink in adults

PINK-FOOTED GOOSE   *Anser brachyrhynchus*

The pink-footed is a small, grey goose with a shorter neck and smaller bill than other grey geese. The bill is fairly dark with a pinkish band near the tip (visible at close range) and the legs and feet are pink. The head and bill usually appear dark brown, contrasting with the paler lower foreflanks and white belly. In flight, the back and wings show grey areas with dark flight feathers.

The pink-footed goose can be distinguished from the bean goose by its shorter neck, rounded head and more delicate bill.

● **SIZE**
Length 60–75cm
(2ft–2ft 6in)

● **BREEDING**
Does not breed in British Isles

● **FOOD**
Roots and leaves, winter stubble

● **HABITAT**
Arctic tundra in summer, coastal marshes, lake margins and fields in winter

● **VOICE**
Musical honking calls and rapid, high-pitched 'wink-wink' call

● **DISTRIBUTION**
Winter visitor from Arctic and Iceland

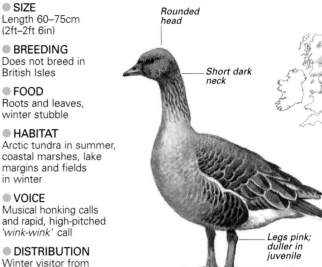

Rounded head

Short dark neck

Legs pink; duller in juvenile

WHITE-FRONTED GOOSE   *Anser albifrons*

Large and greyish brown, the white-fronted goose has a white forehead and orange legs and feet. The adult's underside is marked with dark bands and patches, and the undertail is white. In flight, the darker forewing distinguishes it from the pink-footed goose. Juvenile birds lack the white forehead and their plumage shows fewer contrasts. The Eurasian subspecies, shown here, has a reddish pink bill.

The white-fronted goose is a nervous bird, ready to take flight at the slightest hint of danger. Flocks feed on low-lying grassland at night if the moon is bright enough.

● **SIZE**
Length 65–78cm
(2ft 2in–2ft 7in)

● **BREEDING**
Does not breed in British Isles

● **FOOD**
Roots, leaves and grain

● **HABITAT**
Arctic tundra in summer; visits coastal marshes and inland water meadows in winter

● **VOICE**
Quarrelsome yapping on ground, musical high-pitched honking in flight

● **DISTRIBUTION**
Winter visitor to Britain in large flocks

Grey-brown plumage with paler barred underparts

Orange legs and feet

White forehead does not extend above eye

EGYPTIAN GOOSE   *Alopochen aegyptiacus*

Closely related to the shelduck, this bird's body is grey-brown or reddish buff. It has a dark brown patch over each eye, a dark collar and a chestnut patch on its belly. Legs and bill are pinkish. In flight, striking white forewing patches are visible on both upper and lower surfaces of wings, and an iridescent green panel can be seen on the inner hindwings.

Egyptian geese are seldom seen far from water, although they often feed in fields. They have an upright stance.

● **SIZE**
Length 65–72cm (2ft 2in–2ft 4in)

● **NEST**
Mound of plant material, placed under cover

● **BREEDING**
8–9 off-white eggs laid in April–May

● **FOOD**
Shoots, leaves, roots and seeds

● **HABITAT**
Arable fields and marshes

● **VOICE**
Mostly silent; occasionally harsh braying, wheezing or cackling call

● **DISTRIBUTION**
Escapes and introductions seen mainly in Norfolk

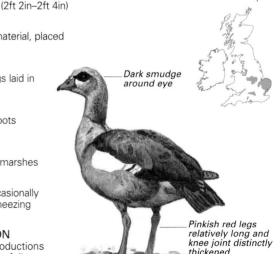

Dark smudge around eye

Pinkish red legs relatively long and knee joint distinctly thickened

The European eel

On rainy nights, mature eels begin their long migration west to the Atlantic Ocean. Masses of them swim down streams and even slither overland through wet grass, flashing silver as they head unerringly for the sea.

Part of the longstanding mystery surrounding eels stemmed from the fact that although adults were plentiful, no larvae or young eels were to be found in British waters. Scientific research has now answered this riddle – no larvae are present because eels do not breed here. Instead, mature eels travel thousands of miles to a remote part of the Atlantic Ocean, where they spawn and then die. How they achieve this feat of navigation remains a subject of debate, but they are uniquely equipped among fish to tackle such a journey.

Also known as the freshwater or yellow eel, the European eel's body is adapted to life in and around lake and river beds. It has one set of paired fins – the pectorals – while the dorsal, tail and anal fins are fused into a continuous median fin along the rear two-thirds of its body.

Eels often burrow into soft sediments and big individuals can even dig tunnels. Unlike most other bony fish, they have almost closed gill chambers with just a tiny slit. This excludes mud and silt from the delicate gill tissues when an eel burrows. It also means that the gills stay moist during overland migrations.

During the day, eels tend to hide in their burrows or among the stones and plants on the lake or river bed, emerging at dusk to hunt for food. Young eels eat a wide variety of invertebrates including worms, insect larvae, snails, mussels and crustaceans, while larger eels tackle small fish and even young ducklings. The eel detects its prey using a sensitive scent organ at the base of two tubular nostrils that emerge from its upper lip. It also eats carrion, which it can smell and home in on from great distances.

Cycle of life

In early autumn, maturing yellow eels start to turn silver. Male eels are almost always less than 50cm (20in) long when they attain sexual maturity, while females are rarely less than that length, and are often considerably larger. The bigger eels are always female because they need to be able to convert their body fat and protein into eggs. Males need fewer nutritional reserves to produce their large numbers of sperm, but both sexes must reserve enough energy to be able to swim all the way to the Sargasso Sea in the western Atlantic, where they spawn. No eels survive to spawn twice. Eel migration peaks each year on dark, usually wet nights, when the first autumn flood waters, or 'spates', occur.

The eels arrive in the Sargasso Sea between February and May when the females release their eggs and the males their sperm. The enormous quantity of eggs – around ten million per female, each egg a millimetre in diameter – allows for the phenomenal mortality that will occur before the survivors return years later to spawn.

The newly hatched larvae feed on planktonic plants and animals as they are carried north and east on the Gulf Stream currents. By the time they reach the continental shelf of Europe, between October and December, they have transformed into tiny, transparent, eel-shaped fish known as 'glass eels'. They subsequently develop a darker coloration along the back and a silvering of the belly, during which time they are called 'elvers'.

The eel's eyesight is different from that of many other predatory fish species, as the retina is rich in the chemical rhodopsin. This gives eels extremely sensitive night vision and enables them to hunt effectively in dark conditions.

SPECIALISATION

Traditionally, eels were split into two categories: wide-mouthed and narrow (or sharp) mouthed forms. It was thought that narrow-snouted individuals specialised in picking out invertebrates from gaps between stones, while wide-mouthed specimens were equipped to engulf larger prey, such as crayfish. Scientists even gave the wide-mouthed form its own specific Latin name – *Anguilla latirostris*.

In subsequent studies, however, a full range of intermediate forms were discovered, revealing that the head shape is simply variable within the species as a whole. This does not preclude the possibility that some individuals are better adapted to one form of feeding strategy than others of a differing shape. Such variation allows the potential for natural selection to confer advantages on certain individuals. Ultimately, perhaps, this may lead to the evolution of genuinely different species.

Several British fish species, such as shad, salmon, sea trout and sea lampreys, spawn in freshwater and undertake the bulk of their growth and maturation at sea – this is known as an anadromous migratory life cycle. The freshwater eel is one of the few species to do the opposite. It spawns at sea and returns as a young eel, or elver, to migrate upstream in search of a home where it can grow to adulthood. This is called a catadromous life cycle.

Mature eels travel a remarkable distance in order to spawn. In the past, the lack of evidence of freshwater spawning by eels led people to postulate (among other things) that eels were spawned from the long hairs of stallions' tails. The truth is only marginally less far-fetched.

After spawning in open water in the Sargasso Sea, the eggs incubate and hatch into tiny transparent leaf-shaped larvae, known as *leptocephali*, which become caught up in the northerly oceanic currents of the Gulf Stream and are swept towards Europe. This journey takes around one year.

It is not known how eel migration evolved to cover thousands of miles. One theory is that millions of years ago eels bred just offshore but continental drift caused the Atlantic Ocean to widen and made the journey longer and longer. It is also not clear how the young eels find their way back to rivers in Europe. To reach these they must pass by Britain, turn east into the Baltic and then migrate south into the German river system.

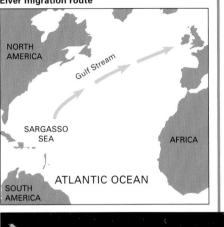

Elver migration route

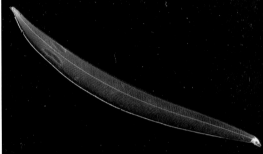

▲ The tiny, flat, leaf-shaped larvae look so different from the other stages of the eel's life cycle that they were once thought to be an entirely different species of fish.

▲ As the elvers move upstream they are exploited by commercial elver netmen on estuaries such as the Severn, as well as by a wide range of predatory fish, mammals and birds.

Elvers are thought to spend about a month adjusting to the brackish waters around estuaries before moving into freshwater when temperatures rise towards 10°C (50°F). From January to June, depending on whether the winter weather has been severe or mild, large numbers of elvers, around 5–10cm (2–4in) long, swarm into estuaries in thick columns, moving over and around obstacles to reach rivers, streams, swamps, pools and lakes. Peak migration tends to occur in late April or May, but stragglers can arrive as late as July or August.

In some river systems, the young eels rest for a while in the lower reaches, with individuals gradually moving further upstream as they grow. In other areas there seems to be a push for the headwaters right from the start.

Small eels have a complex ecology – even their sex is not determined until they reach their destination because it is dependent on the abundance of food. Poor feeding may mean individuals develop into males; well-fed eels tend to become females. Since it is impossible to sex tiny eels, ecologists do not

know for certain but it seems that downstream habitats are occupied by large numbers of small, predominantly male eels, while the longer-lived, larger-growing females often seem to move a long way upstream to mature in higher altitude wetlands.

Freshwater phase

European eels can live in all types of freshwater throughout Britain, provided that they can find a way in. On warm, damp nights young eels wriggle up damp ditches and drains and across wet meadows in search of new homes. Many fall prey to herons, which wait at likely sites for such a meal to come along.

Sometimes eels find themselves effectively landlocked in remote pools without ready access to a river that will allow downstream migration. In this case, eels can spend from a few years to several decades in freshwater before finding a way to the sea.

Individuals can grow to huge sizes in freshwater. Faster growth occurs in richer, warmer, southerly lowland habitats.

The heart, spine and gills are clearly visible in glass eels. Once they start to develop yellowy brown pigmentation, they begin to look more like river eels. At this stage most move upstream to live in freshwater, but some remain in estuaries.

EUROPEAN EEL FACT FILE

When an adult reaches sexual maturity and is ready to migrate to the spawning grounds, its normally dark grey or greenish brown upperside and yellow underside turn silvery grey. Hence the name change from yellow eel to silver eel. Even the size of the eyes and mouth and the shape of the head changes.

● **NAMES**
Common names: eel, freshwater eel, astan, snotty, snake, grig, frogmouth, glut, bulldog, gorb eel, bootlace, yellow eel, silver eel
Scientific name: *Anguilla anguilla*

● **HABITAT**
Rivers, lakes, ponds, ditches, marshes, estuaries; migrate to coastal waters and eventually the Sargasso Sea

● **DISTRIBUTION**
Throughout British Isles

● **STATUS**
Despite some recent declines, eels are still very common and are commercially one of the most important European freshwater fish

● **SIZE**
Female length up to 140cm (4ft 7in), males up to 50cm (20in); weight averages 3–6kg (6½–13lb); record is 12kg (26lb) for an eel that was over 1.5m (5ft) long

● **KEY FEATURES**
Elongated, cylindrical shape; adults dark brown along back, yellower below; dorsal and anal fins extend along body to join tail fin; changes on downstream migration to grey upperside and silver belly with large eyes, small mouth and more pointed head

● **HABITS**
Bottom dwelling, nocturnal, hunt by smell, burrow during day; migrate long distances as elvers and silver eels

● **FOOD**
Insect larvae, worms, snails, crustaceans, crayfish, frogs, tadpoles, fish eggs, young fish, ducklings, carrion

● **BREEDING**
Spawn in the Sargasso Sea in late winter or spring; each female produces around ten million eggs, over which males release sperm; both adults die

● **YOUNG**
Larvae flat, leaf-shaped, 6mm (¼in) long, grow to 75mm (3in) before becoming glass eels, when heart, gills and bones are visible in transparent body; develop into elvers and acquire yellow-brown pigment on moving upstream

Eels use a pair of tube-like nostrils on the upper lip to scent prey. Their eyes are small and covered with a thick transparent skin that separates the eyeball from the surrounding water or air, preventing damage to the eyes when the eel is out of water.

Distribution map key

Present all year round

Not present

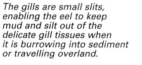

Yellow eels develop larger eyes, smaller mouths and more pointed heads when they are ready to migrate downstream to their marine spawning grounds.

The gills are small slits, enabling the eel to keep mud and silt out of the delicate gill tissues when it is burrowing into sediment or travelling overland.

Solid muscle in the long sinuous body enables the eel to swim strongly against the currents of rivers and to wriggle over land.

A single median fin extends almost the length of the body to join the tail fin. It is supported by over 1000 bony rays.

The pectoral fins are small and used for steering rather than propulsion.

An adult has dark brown upperparts grading into a paler yellowish belly.

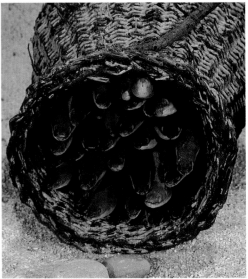

◄ Eels are unusual, and not just because of their shape. Unlike most other bony fish, they have no pelvic fins; neither do they have scales, just smooth, soft skin.

▲ Eel traps and nets are operated on many river and lake systems to take advantage of the annual migration of silver eels – the fish are in prime condition and nutritious prior to spawning. Many thousands of tonnes of silver eels are caught each year.

In cool, upland water, active growth may be possible for just a few weeks of the year, so eels tend to grow more slowly and have longer life spans.

While Irish eels tend to mature after around ten years in freshwater, fish from cold northerly habitats can be 50 years old. A famous eel named 'Putte' was caught as an elver in 1863 and kept in an aquarium at Halsingborg Museum in Sweden, where she lived for 85 years. Studies of eels in Lake Windermere have shown that typical growth is to 10cm (4in) long in one year, 28cm (11in) in five years, 50cm (1ft 8in) in 10 years and up to 100cm (3ft 3in) in 20 years.

Since eels live for so long in freshwater, they are a useful barometer of pollutants, such as pesticides, which can build up in their fatty tissues. Where pollution levels are high, animals such as otters – which eat a lot of eels – can suffer poisoning to the point where their reproductive success can be seriously impaired. The process is called 'bioaccumulation' and is used by environmentalists as evidence of the detrimental effects of pollutants in rivers and streams.

WILDLIFE WATCH

Where can I see eels?

● In autumn, adult eels migrate down streams and rivers; many are caught in traps. During warm, thundery weather, they can sometimes be seen swimming in pools and rivers and, rarely, crossing wet meadows at night.

● Elvers may be seen in rock pools and around weirs near the mouths of rivers. The best time to look for them is probably in March and April as they migrate upstream.

● Maturing eels at the 'yellow' stage of life may be found hiding under debris in muddy rivers and ponds.

A slimy coat of mucus helps eels to survive out of water for long periods without drying out. During overland travels, they breathe aerated water carried in their gill chambers. They can wriggle over land from one stretch of water to another and often occur in landlocked lakes.

White-clawed crayfish

From under stones and out of holes in the banks of clear, fast-flowing streams, white-clawed crayfish venture out cautiously in search of food or even a mate.

Largest of Britain's native freshwater crustaceans is the white-clawed crayfish, *Austropotamobius pallipes*, also known as the Atlantic stream crayfish. Thirty years ago, these animals were commonly found hiding under stones in fast-flowing rivers and streams but the species went into sharp decline and since 1981 has been protected by law.

The main reason for this dramatic decrease was the introduction of the red-clawed North American signal crayfish, *Pacifastacus leniusculus*. Along with several other species, this was brought in to supply the restaurant trade, but inevitably some of the imported fish escaped and the signal crayfish turned out to be a carrier of the deadly crayfish plague, which is caused by a fungus, *Aphanomyces astaci*.

While the signal crayfish suffers no ill effects, the native variety has no natural immunity. Crayfish plague can kill all the white-clawed crayfish in a stream over a period of a few days and has devastated stocks in Italy, France, central Europe, Scandinavia and Siberia, as well as in Britain and Ireland. Moreover, the white-clawed crayfish is threatened by direct competition for food and shelter from the larger and more aggressive signal crayfish, which also produce more young.

Tough shell

Crayfish have both a hard outer skeleton or shell, made of the protein chitin, and an internal skeleton. During their first three or four years, the fish grow rapidly through a series of moults. They neatly shed the old outer skeleton, allowing the new, soft shell to expand and then harden into a protective case. The young crayfish reach around 2cm (1in) after one year, 5cm (2in) after two years, 7cm (3in) at three, up to a maximum of 12cm (5in). After that, the moult is annual. All crustaceans are vulnerable while in soft-shelled phases and cannibalism is common at this time.

The part of the shell that covers the back of the animal, the carapace, encloses a complex series of gills. Provided these gills are kept moist, crayfish are capable of travelling over wet grassland, water meadows, ditches and similar damp country to establish new populations. However, this does not appear to happen very often and reintroduced crayfish take many years to colonise new areas.

▶ Newly hatched young are protected by the female for around ten days. Crayfish mate in the autumn and the female carries the eggs through the winter.

▼ As darkness falls, a crayfish emerges from its sheltered resting place to scavenge for snails, larvae and dead or dying fish. It catches its prey in its powerful claws.

WHITE-CLAWED CRAYFISH FACT FILE

Related to the marine lobster and the crawfish, the white-clawed crayfish uses its two pairs of antennae, the first small and inconspicuous, the second very long and noticeable, to probe its surroundings. They mate in the autumn and the young hatch the following spring.

● **NAMES**
Common names:
white-clawed crayfish,
Atlantic stream crayfish
Scientific name:
Austropotamobius pallipes

● **HABITAT**
Clear, shallow, fast-flowing
streams and rivers, as well as
lakes and ponds

● **DISTRIBUTION**
Mainly in the western half of
England, eastern Wales and
central Ireland

● **STATUS**
Declining

● **SIZE**
Up to 12cm (5in) long, but
mostly less than 10cm (4in)

● **KEY FEATURES**
Carapace olive-green to
brown; 5 pairs of walking
legs, first pair modified into
large claws

● **HABITS**
Shy and often nocturnal;
hides during day; usually
hunts and scavenges at night;
moults periodically

● **FOOD**
Water plants, algae, larvae,
snails, fish

● **BREEDING**
Usually mates in late autumn;
male attaches packets of
sperm to female's underside
using specially modified legs;
eggs carried by female over
winter

● **YOUNG**
Similar to adults but with
domed carapace; cling to
mother's swimmerets for
about 10 days, then become
independent

Clumps of around 200 eggs hang in
clusters from bristles on the swimmerets
located beneath the female's abdomen.

The tailfan
enables the
crayfish
to move
backwards
speedily.

The abdomen
is segmented.

Under the carapace,
the thorax and head
are segmented.

The female's
swimmerets
shield newly
hatched young.

Large claws, paler below than
above and usually whitish or
pale pinkish on the underside.

Distribution map key

Present all year round

Not present

The crayfish's sedentary habits may stem partly from its efforts to avoid danger – crayfish are eaten by eels, pike, trout, mink, otters, herons and humans.

As a deft escape mechanism, the fish has a tailfan that can be flapped rapidly to propel the creature backwards, away from danger. Crayfish swim using a series of short swimming legs, known as swimmerets or 'pleopods', which beat rhythmically beneath the abdomen.

Varied diet
Crayfish are voracious feeders, eating water plants and algae, as well as dead and dying organisms and anything else that they can grasp with their powerful claws, or 'chelipeds'. They use the claws to tear up their food before transferring it to the mouth for chewing. An internal grinding mechanism, known as a 'gastric mill', breaks it down further.

PROTECTED!

The white-clawed crayfish is listed
under Schedule 5 of the Wildlife and
Countryside Act, 1981. It is illegal to kill,
collect or disturb them.

► **Crayfish fight aggressively for space on
stream beds and often lose limbs during
combat. These are gradually regenerated
through a series of moults until the original
function of the lost appendage is restored.**

The pearl mussel

Hunted almost to extinction, this freshwater mussel is now a rare and precious creature in Britain. It may still sometimes be seen burrowed into the silt of clean, fast-flowing rivers.

This freshwater mollusc may be found from Iceland and Lapland down to Portugal and across Russia to Japan, but despite being so widespread it is now extremely rare in Britain.

The pearl mussel (*Margaritifera margaritifera*) has a soft body that is held within a pair of elongated, kidney-shaped shells – or valves – that are yellowish brown when the mussel is young and darken to almost black as it ages. In fast-flowing rivers, it can grow up to 12cm (5in) or more in length. The heavily armoured shells are normally held tightly shut by strong internal muscles. As another safety measure it burrows into the sediment, so that most of its shell is effectively underground with just the tips left exposed. In this way pearl mussels stay out of reach of most predators, except large fish, such as roach, dace and eels, which can dig them up with their snouts.

PEARL FISHING

In Roman times British rivers were renowned for freshwater pearls obtained from the pearl mussel. Pearls are formed within the mantle cavity of a mussel when a tiny piece of grit becomes stuck between the folds of tissue. The vast majority of such foreign bodies are readily flushed out, but if this fails, the mussel responds by secreting layers of shell around the grit, forming 'mother of pearl' or 'nacre'. This gradually builds up into the translucent ball we call a natural pearl. The process occurs in many mussel species, but pearl mussels seem to form pearls more often than others. Perhaps this is because they like to burrow in the sandy beds of large, fast-flowing rivers, while other mussel species live in less turbulent conditions and among softer sediments.

Once plentiful in low-calcium river systems, the pearl mussel is now a rarity in the British Isles. This is mainly due to over-fishing of the mussels for pearls rather than for food. Since pearl mussels are long-lived creatures – pearls take a long time to form – excessive fishing was bound to cause a problem. Pearl mussels are now fully protected.

▲ **When the shells of dead pearl mussels are cleaned and examined, a coating of mother of pearl – the same material from which pearls are formed – can be seen in the inner surface. The outer surface is rough and dull in appearance.**

As with other molluscs, the pearl mussel moves around by extending a muscular 'foot', which emerges from between the two shells. The foot probes the sediments to gain purchase and then pulls the rest of the animal along. The foot is also used for digging.

Filter feeding
Like its marine relatives, the pearl mussel extracts food items from the large volumes of water it pumps between its shells. The water currents are generated by contractions of the muscular mantle, and via the synchronised beating of thousands of tiny hairs called 'cilia'. Several litres of water may pass through the pearl mussel every hour, allowing it to live in places where food is sparse.

As well as food, the mussel also extracts oxygen from the water, which flows over a large area of gills. This is how respiration

PROTECTED!

The freshwater mussel was given full legal protection in 1998, when it was moved on to Schedule 5 of the Wildlife and Countryside Act, 1981. It is illegal to kill, damage or move these animals, or to harm their habitats.

When disturbed or removed from its natural environment, the pearl mussel keeps its two shell valves firmly clamped shut. Only when safely buried in silt will the animal part the valves and begin feeding again.

▲ Just occasionally, living pearl mussels can be seen in clear water after having been dislodged from the sediment. Disturbance is often caused by people or boats.

◄ The presence of a bed of feeding pearl mussels is betrayed by a light swirl of sediment that passes out through the exhalant siphon of each animal. Particles of food will already have been filtered out from the flow of water.

takes place. The narrow shell tips are fringed with sensory tentacles that filter particles flowing into the inhalant siphon. These tentacles keep most of the gritty and inedible particles out, while nutritious algae, bacteria and decaying organic matter called 'detritus' is allowed in. Inside the mantle cavity, an intricate filtering mechanism transports the food to the mussel's mouth.

Freshwater challenge

Most two-shelled, or bivalved, molluscs are marine. Few groups have managed to establish themselves in freshwater environs. Unlike marine mussel larvae, which can drift in the rich plankton, the larvae of freshwater species would normally be swept away from the areas where adults can live. However, freshwater mussels have evolved an extraordinary solution to this problem.

They spawn huge numbers of eggs – up to two million per female. After fertilisation – the male releases sperm into the water and the female takes it in via her inhalant siphon – the eggs are brooded within the gills for several months and grow into tiny bivalved larvae known as 'glochidia'. These are ejected through the exhalant siphon and fall on to the river bed. When a fish swims close by, the larvae instinctively 'clap' their shells together, propelling themselves towards the fish. At the same time a tiny gelatinous thread is expelled which, if they are lucky, will stick to the fish. The larvae climb up the thread and burrow under the skin or gills of the fish, which then acts as a host for the next few weeks of the mussel's life cycle.

A small bump forms round each larva. A fish swimming through a mussel bed can be heavily infested – 5,000 larvae have been counted on a single perch, although they usually live on sea trout, brown trout or juvenile salmon. After a while, the larvae drop off, having transformed into tiny mussels, and colonise new areas.

Rivers with a low calcium content, such as this one in Wales, once supported many freshwater pearl mussels, but numbers have plummeted due to loss of habitat, pollution and illegal fishing.

WILDLIFE WATCH

Where can I see pearl mussels?

● Freshwater mussels are now so rare their beds are best left entirely undisturbed. They are most likely to be in silty or sandy areas of fast-flowing river beds, and only in the north and west of Britain. If you do spot tips of paired shells protruding, take great care and do not attempt to touch – for safety's sake and because the pearl mussel is protected by law.

● You may find an old shell of a dead mussel at the water's edge. The inner surface comprises a series of growth rings similar to those found on a section of tree trunk. Each group of rings corresponds to one year's growth – usually a number of more widely spaced summer growth rings followed by a few closely spaced autumn/winter rings when growth slows or stops. By counting the ring groups, the age of the mussel when it died can be estimated. Freshwater mussels can live for up to 120 years.

Mosquitoes

In damp, warm weather, mosquitoes are busy laying their eggs in ditches, ponds and other areas of standing water and this is when the females are most likely to bite.

Reviled for their habit of biting humans, mosquitoes are slender flies that belong to the family Culicidae. Often called gnats in Britain, they can be distinguished from several superficially similar groups of flies by their piercing mouthparts and the presence of scales on their wing veins.

About 30 species of mosquito live in the British Isles. A microscope is needed to identify most of them, but some can be recognised with the naked eye by the arrangement of pale bands on the legs and abdomen. The banded mosquito, *Culiseta annulata*, is one these, with spotted wings and strongly banded legs and abdomen. Britain's largest mosquito, its body can reach a length of 8mm (almost ⅜in). Some male mosquitoes can also be recognised by the shape of their palps (mouthparts), which are often noticeably curved and decorated with tufts of hair.

The whine produced by the rapidly beating wings of a female mosquito is an alarming sound to most humans, but to a male mosquito it is an irresistible mating

An adult mosquito breaks free of its protective pupal case and rests for a moment on the water's surface. It will fly away once its wings have expanded and hardened. Most adult males live for just a few days.

call. He picks up the vibrations with his bushy antennae and follows them until he reaches the female. Slightly different flight tones ensure that males are not attracted to females of another species.

In search of blood

Although most female mosquitoes need a drink of blood before they can lay their eggs, their main source of food is energy-rich nectar from flowers. When she needs to take a meal of blood, a female mosquito uses a combination of scent and warmth to home in on a suitable victim.

A female banded mosquito's abdomen swells as she extracts a meal of blood. She injects saliva containing an anti-clotting agent and this causes the itching sensation.

She then explores the host's skin with the tip of her modified mouthparts before drawing back the sheath around them to expose her needle-like jaws. Six needles fit together to form a canal through which the blood is syringed. At the same time, the mosquito injects saliva into the wound and this is what makes the bite itch so much, although some people are far more sensitive than others.

Not all mosquitoes are attracted to humans. Several species prefer birds, and male mosquitoes never bite – they lack piercing mouthparts and eat only nectar.

Mosquitoes spend all of their early lives in water. *Culex pipiens*, the most common species, is one of several that breeds in garden ponds, water butts or wherever

MALARIA

Malaria is the most widespread and serious of the many diseases carried by mosquitoes. Only individuals of the genus *Anopheles* can carry it because the malaria parasite cannot complete its life cycle in other species. Malaria affects millions of people every year in warmer parts of the world. In the past, a mild form of malaria, known as ague, occurred throughout low-lying areas of Britain and some species are still capable of transmitting the disease.

▲ Most mosquito larvae hang from the surface of the water, breathing through their tails and feeding by filtering the water for planktonic plant life. One larva here is larger than the rest and will pupate first.

there is standing water. Other mosquitoes are more choosy – several breed just in brackish water, while others will lay their eggs only in water-filled tree holes in woodlands. Females usually lay their eggs on the water surface.

Hanging around

Mosquito larvae have large heads and slender bodies. They feed on bacteria and other microscopic organisms, which they waft into their mouths with moustache-like tufts of hair. After three moults, and as little as 10 days in warm weather, the larvae are ready to pupate. The comma-shaped pupae of most species hang at an angle from the surface film and breathe air through little breathing tubes or 'horns'. *Anopheles* larvae are an exception. These lie horizontally just below the surface and have no breathing tubes. Unlike most pupae, those of mosquitoes are very mobile and if disturbed they will wriggle rapidly into the depths. The pupal stage generally lasts up to four or five days, after which the adult insect breaks out at the water surface. It clings to its pupal skin for perhaps a minute or two while its wings expand, and then flies away.

Some species of mosquito, such as *Aedes caspius*, breed twice a year; others, such as *Culex pipiens*, breed many times. During the autumn, however, the females do not lay their eggs but seek damp, sheltered places, such as cellars and drains, in which to spend the winter. Some become completely dormant, while others wake periodically and seek blood meals. A winter bite is usually from *Culiseta annulata*, although in coastal areas it could be *Anopheles atroparvus*, which breeds in brackish water.

A swarm of mating mosquitoes, a fairly common sight in summer, may still be seen on a warm evening in early autumn.

▲ The common mosquito lays around 300 eggs that form a raft on any body of still water, from an abandoned bucket to a pond or ditch. The eggs float until they hatch into tiny larvae, around 48 hours later.

WILDLIFE WATCH

How can I learn more about mosquitoes?

● A good way to study mosquitoes is to collect some larvae from a pond. Put them in a small fish tank half full with water but with no fish, and with a layer of organic debris at the bottom; make sure the tank has a cover.

● Watch the larvae feeding and turning into pupae and, later, the amazing transformation as the pupae hatch into adult insects at the surface.

Water fleas

These minute creatures play an important role in freshwater ecosystems, where they feed on algae and in turn provide food for insects, fish and ducks.

▲ In ideal conditions water fleas can multiply very quickly to form dense populations. A cubic metre of lake water may contain many thousands of them.

▶ An intricate arrangement of filtering bristles allows the water flea to recognise edible fragments of food, such as bacteria, algae and small pieces of decaying organic matter known as 'detritus'. These are swallowed while inedible particles are ejected.

L ook at water fleas under a microscope and it is easy to see why they are so named. The body shape and the way they appear to 'jump' or move jerkily through the water resemble the shape and movement of fleas. However, these tiny, almost transparent creatures are actually crustaceans. They belong to a group known as cladocerans, of which the *Daphnia* species is among the most common. *Daphnia* often form dense swarms at differing depths in lakes, corresponding to available food sources.

Since water fleas can rapidly become very numerous, they exert a powerful influence on populations of algae and bacteria (known as 'phytoplankton'), eating so many that they keep the water relatively clear. In places where there are plenty of fish that consume *Daphnia* in large quantities, algal populations can increase dramatically, especially if nutrient levels in the water are high. This can lead to unattractive pea-green, soupy water choked with a so-called 'algal bloom' that shades out any submerged plants.

In the Norfolk Broads, fish have been removed from rivers to help re-establish dense *Daphnia* populations, which in turn have cleared the algal blooms. In a natural lake ecosystem, a peak or a trough of algal and bacterial productivity will be followed by a rise or a fall in the population of *Daphnia* and other planktonic crustaceans, so the water clarity remains fairly evenly balanced.

The character of these planktonic crustaceans is profoundly affected by levels of fish predation. Where this is commonplace, the crustacean community tends to comprise small, agile,

clear-bodied species, many of which may be active at night. Where fish predation pressure is low or absent, larger, slow-moving species such as *Daphnia magna* thrive. However, these larger species are not necessarily safe because they are a major food source for filter-feeding ducks, such as the shoveler.

Reproductive strategies

Many species of water flea have the ability to reproduce either sexually or asexually. In asexual reproduction, females give birth to further females without their eggs being fertilised by males.

WATER FLEA FACT FILE

Encased within a pair of shell-like valves and sporting outsize antennae, these tiny crustaceans swim in ditches, ponds and backwaters. Most feed by filtering out algae and other tiny particles. The distinct head has large, dark eyes that react to varying light levels.

● **NAMES**
Common name: water flea
Scientific names: genera *Daphnia*,
Simocephalus and *Leptodora*

● **HABITAT**
Freshwater

● **DISTRIBUTION**
Throughout British Isles

● **STATUS**
Very common in most of its wide range

● **SIZE**
Up to 1cm (½in) long, depending on species

● **KEY FEATURES**
Small, superficially flea-like, aquatic crustaceans; body pale with blackish eyes and green-brown gut

● **HABITS**
Swims jerkily using large, branched antennae; adults live for just a few weeks; dormant eggs can survive many years

● **FOOD**
Freshwater algae, bacteria, detritus

● **BREEDING**
Combination of asexual and sexual reproduction, dictated by environmental conditions

● **YOUNG**
Produces 20 or more eggs at a time, which hatch in a day or so; young are miniature adults

Distribution map key

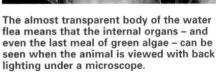

▨ Present all year round

☐ Not present

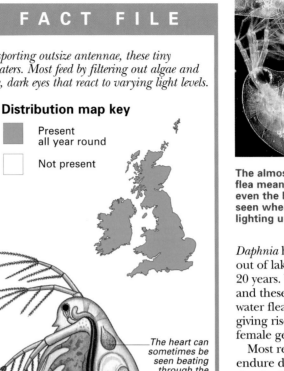

A pair of large antennae are used for swimming.

The heart can sometimes be seen beating through the translucent valves and body wall.

Eggs develop in a brood pouch that occupies most of the female's body.

The almost transparent body of the water flea means that the internal organs – and even the last meal of green algae – can be seen when the animal is viewed with back lighting under a microscope.

Daphnia have been successfully hatched out of lake bed mud that has been dry for 20 years. When conditions have improved and these 'resting' eggs hatch, the young water fleas go on to reproduce asexually, giving rise to further parthenogenetic female generations.

Most resting eggs do not have to endure drying or freezing, however, and simply allow the water flea population to overwinter when food supplies tend to be restricted. These little creatures are very well adapted to survive the vagaries of aquatic ecosystems.

The process is called 'parthenogenesis'. Parthenogenetic reproduction occurs during most of the year, from spring to autumn, when planktonic population levels tend to increase and decline rapidly in response to food supply, weather and predation. For water fleas living in relatively large, stable lakes, this accounts for virtually all reproductive activity.

However, when adverse environmental conditions occur, especially in winter, some eggs hatch as males, and females start to produce eggs that require fertilisation. These dark-coloured eggs are shed in a protective case that makes them resistant to drying out or freezing, which enables water-flea populations to survive even the drying out of their habitat. Remarkably, species such as

WILDLIFE WATCH

Where can I see water fleas?

● Look carefully in ditches, ponds and lake margins to see swarms of yellowish green or reddish Daphnia swimming around. They are so nutritious that it is commonplace to see various fish cruising open-mouthed through the water, taking advantage of an easy source of food.

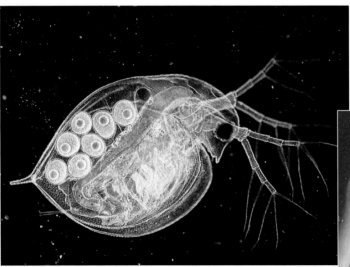

▲ In favourable conditions, water fleas reproduce at a great rate. Unfertilised eggs develop within the brood pouch of females. Each has a yolk large enough to sustain the developing young.

▶ Young water fleas develop in an internal brood pouch until they are ready to fend for themselves as miniature adults.

◀ In times of hardship water flea populations prepare for the worst by producing highly resilient 'resting' eggs. These eggs do not hatch inside the female, but are released into the water. They may lie dormant in pond sediment for months or years, until conditions improve enough to support a new generation.

Bulrushes and bur-reeds

Giant, grass-like fronds of bulrushes and the related bur-reeds line many wild watercourses. Waterfowl seek shelter in the thick stands of vegetation and feed on the plants' seedheads.

The bulrush is a majestic waterside plant, growing up to 3m (10ft) tall. It forms extensive stands along the margins of lakes and slow-flowing rivers.

Marshes and shallow water around the margins of lakes, pools and slow-flowing rivers are where bulrushes (or reedmace) and bur-reed grow. These tall, reed-like perennials belong to two separate but closely related families – the Typhaceae and Sparganiaceae.

Bulrushes spread by means of rhizomes (creeping horizontal stems) and can form extensive patches. Their numerous leaves are flat, sword-like and hairless, and their sheathed, stout, erect stems bear sausage-like flower clusters near the tips. Tiny female flowers are packed into a cylindrical brown cluster, with male flowers in a looser spike above them at the very tip of the stem.

The flowers are wind-pollinated, and the petals and outer flower parts, or sepals, are mere hairs. The male flowers have one to three stamens and the female flowers have a single ovule that, by early autumn, develops into a single-seeded fruit, which splits when ripe. The flower clusters gradually break up and eventually the seeds drift away, carried on the wind by the hair-like flower parts.

Bur-reeds are smaller than bulrushes, with shorter rhizomes and mainly branched stems. The leaves, which are narrow, pointed and hairless, sometimes float on the water's surface. The tiny flowers are massed in spherical heads, which are loosely arranged on the branches and resemble miniature candelabras. The male heads are smaller and mounted on the stalk above the female flowerheads.

Bur-reeds have between one and six scale-like sepals and petals. The male flowers have one to eight pale yellow stamens and the female flowers usually have a single ovule. The head develops into a neat, spiky, burr-like cluster of dry, one-seeded nutlets, from which the name bur-reed is derived. The outer layer of the nutlet is spongy, allowing dispersal via water, and waterfowl eat huge numbers of nutlets, dispersing the seeds in their droppings.

Sweet-flag

A waterside plant similar to bulrushes and bur-reeds, sweet-flag is distinguished by its aromatic leaves, which smell of tangerine and vanilla when crushed. The leaves have crinkled margins and horn-like clusters of tiny, green flowers. A member of the arum family, Araceae, sweet-flag was introduced from Turkey in the 16th century and was often strewn over church floors. Its distribution is uneven but it is common in some places, in particular the Norfolk Broads.

BULRUSH OR REEDMACE?

According to strict botanical nomenclature, the name 'bulrush' refers to another plant – the common clubrush, *Scirpus lacustris*. Purists much prefer the name 'reedmace' for *Typha latifolia,* which avoids any confusion. The name bulrush, which is now widely used, probably originated from Victorian illustrations that misleadingly depicted Moses in his basket by the Nile among stands of *Typha.*

Lesser bulrush or lesser reedmace
Typha angustifolia

Bulrush, great reedmace or cat's-tail
Typha latifolia

◄ The seedheads of bulrushes appear in summer, but do not shed their seeds until the following February. Then the closely packed flowers dry out, and the hair-like petals and sepals form a mass of soft down that is carried off by the wind.

Sweet-flag
Acorus calamus

► The yellowish green flower-cones of sweet-flag protrude from among its long leaves. This water plant flowers infrequently and fruiting is unknown.

BULRUSH FACT FILE

● **Bulrush, great reedmace or cat's-tail**
Typha latifolia
Habitat and distribution
Widespread and locally common in mineral-rich water of shallow lakes, ponds, ditches, canals and slow-moving rivers; scarce in Scotland
Size 1–3m (3–10ft 3in) tall
Key features
Clump-forming perennial with creeping rhizomes; leaves greyish green, long, flat, sword-like, 18–24mm (¾–1in) wide; female flowers massed in sausage-like heads 18–30mm (¾–1¼in) wide, male flowers in narrower cluster above
Flowering time
June–August; seedheads remain through autumn and winter

● **Lesser bulrush or lesser reedmace**
Typha angustifolia
Habitat and distribution
Similar habitats to bulrush, especially on coasts, but less tolerant of polluted waters; rare in Wales, Scotland and Ireland

Size 1–3m (3–10ft 3in) tall
Key features
Similar to bulrush but leaves green, about 5mm (¼in) wide; male and female flower clusters separated by short but distinct length of bare stem; female flower clusters about 10mm (½in) wide
Flowering time
June–July

● **Sweet-flag**
Acorus calamus
Habitat and distribution
Found in shallow, nutrient-rich or calcareous water at margins of ponds, canals and rivers on muddy soils, mostly in England
Size 60–120cm (2–4ft) tall
Key features
Clump-forming perennial with creeping rhizomes; leaves bright green, smell of tangerines and vanilla when bruised, long, flat, sword-like, 15–20mm (½–¾in) wide with crinkled margins; flowers in green, horn-like masses towards top of stems
Flowering time
June–July

▲ The flowering heads of bur-reeds are important in autumn and winter as a source of food for wildfowl. The seeds are subsequently dispersed in the birds' droppings.

▲ Branched bur-reed grows alongside ponds and waterways throughout Britain. Its dense stands provide valuable cover for nesting and roosting birds.

BUR-REED FACT FILE

● **Branched bur-reed**
Sparganium erectum
Habitat and distribution
Widespread and common on damp ground and in shallow water at edges of lakes, ponds, streams, canals and ditches. Not found in north-east Scotland or Ireland
Size 40–150cm (1ft 4in–5ft) tall
Key features
Tufted perennial with erect, branched stems; leaves mostly basal, about 10–15mm (⅝in) wide, pointed, keeled near base; flowers grouped in conspicuous dense, round heads, each branch with many male clusters near tip, 1–3 female clusters at base; fruit clusters up to 25mm (1in) across
Flowering time
June–August

● **Unbranched bur-reed**
Sparganium emersum
Habitat and distribution
Shallow water of rivers, canals, streams, lakes and ponds, especially in England
Size 30–60cm (1–2ft) tall
Key features
Similar to branched bur-reed; leaves narrower, floating, keeled beneath; flowers in 3–7 male and 3–4 stalked or stalkless female clusters; fruit clusters up to 20mm (¾in) across
Flowering time
June–August

● **Floating bur-reed**
Sparganium angustifolium
Habitat and distribution Acid, peaty mountain lochs and pools; frequent on Scottish islands, scarce in north-western England, western and South Wales, New Forest and Ireland
Size Stems up to 60cm (2ft) long
Key features
Similar to unbranched bur-reed, but stems weak, submerged or floating; leaves flat, grass-like; flowers in 2 male and 2–4 stalked female clusters; fruit clusters up to 15mm (⅝in) across
Flowering time
June–August

● **Least bur-reed or small bur-reed**
Sparganium natans
Habitat and distribution
Shallow margins of acid or alkaline lakes and pools with peaty bottoms, mainly in Scotland and Ireland
Size Stems up to 30cm (1ft) long
Key features
Similar to unbranched bur-reed, but stems and leaves floating; leaves narrower, flat; flowers in only 1 male and 2–4 stalkless or short-stalked female clusters; fruiting clusters 10mm (½in) across
Flowering time
June–August

▶ A plant of peaty mountain lochs and pools, floating bur-reed is a distinctly localised species, found mainly in northern Scotland and Ireland.

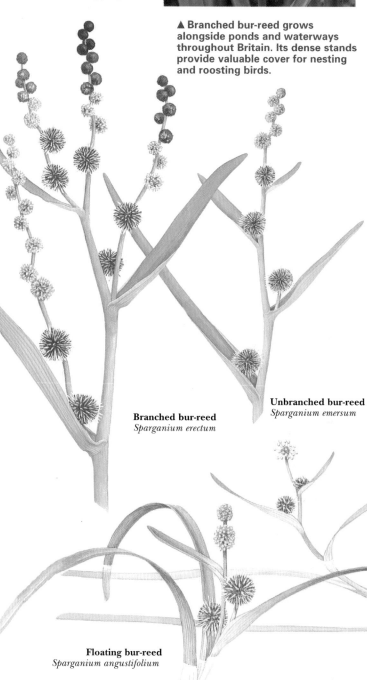

Branched bur-reed
Sparganium erectum

Unbranched bur-reed
Sparganium emersum

Least bur-reed or small bur-reed
Sparganium natans

Floating bur-reed
Sparganium angustifolium

WILDLIFE WATCH

Where do bulrushes and bur-reeds grow?

● Bulrushes form clumps and beds by lakes and ponds, and along the margins of slow-flowing rivers and canals. Sweet-flag is common in parts of East Anglia.

● Bur-reeds are widespread in marshy ground, beside ponds and slow-flowing streams. Floating bur-reed and least bur-reed occur mainly in the peaty waters of northern Scotland and Ireland.

The balsams

When many wild flowers have died away, the balsams are still displaying their brightly coloured blooms. Any stretch of waterway may harbour a bankside colony.

There are four species of balsam growing wild in Britain but only one of them, touch-me-not balsam, is native. The rest are garden escapes that have become naturalised over the last two centuries. They all belong to the genus *Impatiens* and have their own family, the Balsaminaceae.

Balsams are rather stout, slightly fleshy, brittle-stemmed and hairless annuals with oval,

elliptical or spear-shaped, toothed leaves, often in opposing pairs. The flowers, which are long-stalked and hang in small clusters, have five petals arranged in an unusual pattern. Four of the petals are fused to form a broad lower lip while the fifth petal forms a small upper hood. The lowermost of the three or five petal-like sepals forms an inflated bag or sac that extends into a curved, nectar-secreting spur.

Seed dispersal

As the club-shaped fruits ripen, tension builds up in their fleshy walls until the slightest touch or vibration causes them to explode. The segments split apart and twist

violently, hurling the numerous seeds 10m (33ft) or more from the parent plant. The light seeds float readily in water, further aiding dispersal.

A long history

Touch-me-not balsam was recorded as long ago as 1632 on the Welsh border in Shropshire, where it still grows today. The similar orange balsam was first recorded in Surrey in 1822 by philosopher John Stuart Mill, who was a keen botanist. It had probably just arrived from North America and soon spread along the recently constructed canal system to as far north as Yorkshire. Small balsam arrived from Russia with timber in the 19th century,

and it readily invaded estate woodland and parks. Today it is a familiar plant, especially in shady gardens in south-eastern Britain.

The most common and conspicuous species, Indian balsam, arrived from the Himalayas in 1839 as a greenhouse plant. It is now widespread, especially in northern England, forming vast banks of colour alongside rivers, canals and streams.

Wildlife trusts and anglers occasionally wage war on this plant, because it easily out-competes more diverse native vegetation. However, it is one of the most handsome wild plants of late summer and autumn, and its flowers attract numerous bees.

▼ Touch-me-not balsam is also known as yellow balsam because of its delicate yellow flowers, which are still to be seen in September.

DID YOU KNOW?

The English name touch-me-not refers to the flower's explosive seed pods. In addition, the Latin name *Impatiens* – which literally means 'impatient' – refers to the way the pods burst violently when ripe, hurling the seeds in the air.

▶ Indian balsam forms dense swards along river banks, where it is pollinated by bumblebees. Bees, in search of nectar, are completely enclosed by the deep flower.

BALSAM FACT FILE

● **Touch-me-not balsam or yellow balsam**
Impatiens noli-tangere
Habitat and distribution
Banks of rivers and streams, and wet woodland in the Lake District, southern fringes of North Wales and Shropshire; locally introduced in southern England
Size 50–100cm (1ft 8in–3ft 3in)
Key features
An erect, branched, hairless annual; flowers yellow, speckled with red or brown spots, hang in clusters of 3–6, up to 35mm (1⅜in) long; sac-like sepal gradually narrows into a downward curved spur; leaves oval or oblong, toothed, stalked, in opposite pairs
Flowering time
July–September

● **Orange balsam or jewel-weed**
Impatiens capensis
Habitat and distribution
Native to eastern North America; increasingly naturalised by rivers and canals in central and southern Britain
Size 30–150cm (1–5ft) tall
Key features
Similar to yellow balsam; flowers orange with large reddish brown blotches; sac-like sepal abruptly narrows into long, crook-like spur; leaves held in alternate pairs
Flowering time
June–August

▲ The attractive flowers of orange balsam hang like tiny orange lanterns. It is not hard to see how the plant acquired its North American name of 'jewel-weed'.

► Orange balsam is to be found alongside canals and on river banks. Its light, corky seeds float well and are easily dispersed.

Touch-me-not balsam or yellow balsam
Impatiens noli-tangere

Orange balsam or jewel-weed
Impatiens capensis

◄ Touch-me-not balsam is a plant of damp woodlands and river banks in parts of the Lake District, North Wales and Shropshire. Elsewhere, it is scattered in small patches.

▲ Small balsam has naturalised in moist, shady places in much of Britain, but is most common in south-eastern England.

▶ Attractive yellow flowers appear on the small balsam from May to September or later. They are pollinated principally by hoverflies.

Small balsam
Impatiens parviflora

▶ Although it is an exotic alien, Indian balsam is popular with many gardeners because of its gorgeous flowers. These range in colour from palest pink to deep claret and are pollinated by bees. The plants are known in some places as 'bee-bums'.

Indian balsam, Himalayan balsam, policeman's helmet or bee-bum
Impatiens glandulifera

WILDLIFE WATCH

Where can I see balsams?

● Balsams grow beside rivers, canals and streams, in damp woodlands and on wasteground. They are all fairly widespread, but only Indian balsam is found in Ireland. They often occur in abundance, forming great swathes of colour.

BALSAM FACT FILE

● **Small balsam**
Impatiens parviflora
Habitat and distribution
Native to central Asia and Siberia; widely but patchily naturalised in damp woodlands, parks and wasteground as far north as the Moray Firth
Size: 20–60cm (8–24in) tall
Key features
An erect, hairless annual; flowers yellow, smaller than other British balsams, up to 18mm (¾in) long; sac-like sepal narrows into a short, straight spur; leaves oval or oblong, saw-toothed, nettle-like, stalked, in alternate pairs
Flowering time
June–November

● **Indian balsam, Himalayan balsam, policeman's helmet or bee-bum**
Impatiens glandulifera
Habitat and distribution
Native to the Himalayas, naturalised on streamsides, river banks and canal banks, in wet woodlands and damp wasteground, especially in central and northern England and Wales; rarer in Scotland
Size: 1–3m (3–10ft 3in) tall
Key features
A tall, erect, hairless annual, with stout, little branched, often reddish stems; strongly scented flowers, up to 40mm (1½in) long, in many shades of pink, sometimes almost white, in clusters; large, sac-like sepal abruptly narrows into a narrow, curved spur; leaves in opposite pairs or triplets, spear-shaped or broadly elliptical, pointed, toothed, each tooth tipped with a small, reddish gland; seeds black
Flowering time
June–October

Coast watch

- The grey seal
- The chough
- The dunlin
- The fulmar
- The mackerel
- Shrimps and prawns
- Common limpets

- Piddocks and shipworms
- Sand hoppers
- Gentians and centauries
- Salt-marsh plants

The grey seal

When these marine mammals gather on shore to breed, they can often be seen in their hundreds at favoured sites, especially around the Scottish islands. Aggressive males vigorously defend their harem against all-comers.

Two-thirds of the world's population of grey seals live around the coast of the British Isles. They spend most of their lives at sea, preferring clear, unpolluted water, but they may be seen every autumn, hauling themselves ashore to breed. They come ashore again for a short while in winter and spring to moult, and in summer they occasionally bask on rocks, resting in the warm sunshine.

Grey seal adults are around 2m (6½ft) long and the male has a horse-like face with a flat forehead that tapers into a long muzzle. The common (or harbour) seal, by contrast, has a rounded head with a small, neat muzzle, and is about half the size. While common seals are fairly evenly distributed around most of the coastline, grey seals are more abundant on northern and western shores.

Breeding season

Grey seals usually come ashore to breed in late September, but it can be as late as November in the Farne Islands, off the coast of Northumberland. They return to traditional breeding grounds, year after year, mainly on remote islands free from disturbance and predators. Mature animals return to beaches where they have successfully raised pups in the past. The oldest females arrive first and their pups, conceived in the previous season's mating, are born soon afterwards.

After giving birth to a single pup each, the females are soon ready to mate again and the adult males start to come ashore. The biggest bulls arrive first, gathering a small cluster of females and defending them against the attentions of rival males. There is no physically defined territory; the area dominated by each bull changes from day to day. Nevertheless, each bull fiercely chases away potential challengers, and sometimes fighting ensues. The whole point of this strenuous activity is for each bull to mate with as many cows as he can in order to father as many pups as possible to carry on his genes. The bull's success depends very much on his size and stamina. Unsuccessful males will be banished to the periphery of the colony or be obliged to stay in the shallows.

The earliest bulls ashore benefit from the dominance this first claim affords

The grey seal lives at relatively high latitudes where little sunlight penetrates the water, so it needs big eyes to see in the gloomy conditions.

them, but it comes at a price. During the breeding period, the bull does not leave his station for fear of being superseded by a rival, enduring up to eight weeks of constant alertness night and day, without going to sea to feed. The earliest bulls to arrive on the beach therefore lose the greatest amount of weight, which takes a heavy toll on their condition.

Survival rates are similar for both sexes up until breeding age, which starts at four to five years for cows and seven to ten years for bulls. After that, however, the males become increasingly worn out with each successive breeding season and their life expectancy is sharply reduced – the larger the number of females and greater breeding success, the shorter the bull's life span may be. Consequently, bull seals rarely live beyond around 20 to 25 years, whereas the cows can still be breeding ten years later.

SEAL SENSES

Seals are well adapted for life in and out of water. Their eyes are able to cope with a wide range of light intensities, having retinas that function well in dimly lit conditions, such as those encountered in the sea. Their ears are also modified to work underwater, with specialised tissues in the auditory canal to adjust the pressure in the ears when diving.

The long whiskers are well supplied with nerve fibres, which indicates that they may be used to detect small movements in the water, possibly caused by prey.

GREY SEAL FACT FILE

A large, dark grey mammal with a tapering body, the grey seal may be seen on or around rocky shores throughout the year. Large groups come ashore for several weeks to produce young, but only on undisturbed islands and remote beaches.

● **NAMES**
Common names: grey seal, Atlantic seal; male is a bull, female a cow
Scientific name: *Halichoerus grypus*

● **HABITAT**
Rocky coasts, especially uninhabited islands and isolated beaches with sea caves

● **DISTRIBUTION**
Mostly around western and northern Scotland, but also Farne Islands and other undisturbed breeding grounds

● **STATUS**
More than 130,000

● **SIZE**
Bulls about 2m (6½ft) long, cows 1.8m (6ft); weight 150–250kg (331–551lb); bull is about 50% heavier than female

● **KEY FEATURES**
Flat forehead and elongated snout; bulls usually dark grey with a few pale patches; cows more variable but generally lighter with pale cream on belly and scattering of dark blotches all over

● **HABITS**
Largely inactive when ashore; at sea, sometimes seen 'bottling' – floating upright in the water with just nostrils above the surface; when feeding, spend 80% of time under water

● **VOICE**
Adults make moaning, hooting, growling and hissing sounds; bulls sometimes make a deep puffing sound a bit like a steam engine; pups squeal

● **FOOD**
Mainly fish from a wide range of species; also crustaceans, squid, octopus and occasionally seabirds

● **BREEDING**
Single pups born late autumn

● **NEST**
No nest; females give birth among rocks and stones, or on sandy beach; occasionally on hillside

● **YOUNG**
Born with thick, white coat; moult to pale grey before going to sea for first time at 8 weeks old

● **SIGNS**
Large brown or grey droppings (often containing fish bones) left on rocks; droppings are bright orange during breeding season

The male grey seal has an elongated snout and distinctive convex profile from the top of the head to the nose, above a wide, heavy muzzle – hence its scientific name 'grypus', meaning hook-nosed.

Distribution map key

Present all year round

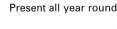

The female has a slender muzzle with a flatter profile than the male. Unlike the common seal, grey seals have nostrils that are clearly separated.

Grey seals come ashore to change their coat once a year, and this takes several weeks. The females moult between January and March and males moult from March to May.

The hind legs form flippers with thick webbing between the toes. The flippers are used for steering rather than propulsion.

Grey seals have been legally protected by their own separate Act of Parliament since 1914. They may not be killed around British coasts between 1 September and 31 December without a licence. The last organised cull in the UK was in 1983.

Baby seals

The young are born weighing about 14kg (31lb), with a thick coat of white fur to protect them from the wind and rain. They cannot swim in this baby coat, so do not enter the water until they have moulted, revealing the adult coat underneath. This consists of special short, stiff hairs that protect the skin from being damaged as the animal heaves itself over rocks.

Insulation is provided by a thick layer of fat under the skin. This builds up rapidly as the pup grows, nourished by its mother's milk. The pup suckles every five hours or so for the first three weeks of its life. After that, the gap increases and the cow is able to return to sea to feed. Curiously, on her return from these forays, she may sometimes feed a pup other than her own. This is presumably by mistake because the females can ill-afford to waste precious milk on the offspring of others. The milk is formed from the mother's own fat reserves, and she loses an average of 3kg (6¼lb) of body weight per day during the suckling period.

Seals produce very creamy milk which is extraordinarily rich in fat (about 55 per cent), assisting the baby to develop its own insulation and also enabling its rapid growth – the pup triples its birthweight in

▲ A grey seal cow gives birth to one pup a year for up to 35 years. The females can live until the age of 45 or more.

► The white baby fur makes a young grey seal very conspicuous on the beach in its first three weeks of life, before the fur is shed.

the first three weeks. This phenomenal weight gain is brought about solely by its mother's nutritious milk.

The mothers do little for their pups except feed them and keep away other seals that might be a nuisance. Towards the end of the suckling period, the cows mate with one or more bulls and then return to the sea. This terminates family life rather suddenly and the pups are abandoned on

the open beach. They go to sea for the first time shortly after this and, at around eight weeks old, must quickly learn to fend for themselves.

Fish eaters

The grey seal's diet is almost entirely made up of fish. An adult takes around 5kg (11lb) per day of the species that are most abundant. This has brought them into conflict with fishermen in some places, such as the Orkney Isles, where they were believed to be responsible for a decline in commercial fish stocks. However, seals also take other, non-commercial species and the effect of their predation may actually be to increase the numbers of larger commercial fish, thereby benefiting fishermen.

Delayed implantation

The gestation period for grey seals lasts about seven months, but they are among a number of British mammals that have delayed implantation. This means that the fertilised egg does not develop immediately after mating. Instead, it enters into a state of suspended development, only implanting into the wall of the womb after a delay of up to four months. This allows the seals to mate when they are all together on the breeding beaches but the pups are not born until eight or so months later. It is perhaps an unusual strategy to give birth at the beginning of winter when storms

THREAT DISPLAY

Each huge bull tries to keep other males away from his own group of cows, fiercely defending his harem, which may number up to ten females. If the beach is not easily accessible, a bull may be able to occupy a strategic position and block others from coming ashore to compete for his females. In such a situation, his harem may be larger than that of other males on more open beaches.

Rival males will be chased away with a noisy display or even active combat. Some of the oldest animals bear many scars around their shoulders as souvenirs of previous encounters, but their skin is specially thickened in such areas so the wounds are superficial.

The loud, bellowing roars made by a male grey seal proclaim his status and warn off rivals. Female grey seals can also be excitable and quite noisy on occasions.

lash the beach. Indeed, common seals wait until the weather is more congenial, breeding and giving birth in summer. Nevertheless, the grey seal's breeding strategy is successful. On average 75 to 85 per cent of pups normally survive to go to sea and, overall, grey seal numbers have been steadily increasing by more than 5 per cent per year in some areas.

Overcrowding problems

One effect of this increase is that seals returning to the same beaches every year have found themselves having to share with ever increasing numbers. This overcrowding has forced some seals to move away from the shore, even on to rocky hillsides up to 80m (260ft) above the sea. Getting to such a height must be a huge effort for these large animals, which otherwise do not move more than a couple of metres from the water's edge.

Some of these hillside sites are far from ideal. The slopes are often covered with soil and when this is churned up by the seals in the autumn rain, it soon turns to mud. Pups born into these messy conditions suffer a high mortality rate and as many as 40 per cent may die. However, the same can be true of pups battered by waves on overcrowded beaches.

Seals have no major predators apart from humans, although they occasionally fall prey to killer whales. Once they leave the breeding beaches, the survival of young seals is remarkably high. About two-thirds of them survive their first year, after which more than 90 per cent survive each subsequent year.

Long-distance swimmers

Little is known about grey seal's behaviour at sea except that they travel long distances and at remarkable speeds. For instance, a pup born on the Isle of May, north of the Farne Islands, was found in Norway just nine days later and must have made the journey at a rate of around 65km (40 miles) a day. Other pups from North Rona, an uninhabited island 130km (80 miles) north-west of Cape Wrath on the north-west Scottish mainland, have turned up in Iceland.

▲ Grey seals prefer to have their young close to the sea, the source of their food, often among rocks and boulders. They do not build nests and muddy or grassy areas are less attractive.

◄ Sea water does not normally freeze around Britain. However, in estuaries where the salt water is more dilute, it can freeze on the seal's whiskers during extremely cold weather.

WILDLIFE WATCH

Where can I see grey seals?

● The best place to see grey seals is the Farne Islands off the coast of Northumberland. Boat trips go from the town of Seahouses in the summer.

● Boats visit Hilbre Island from Thurstaston in the Wirral, Cheshire. Seal watching boat trips are available from various places around Cornwall.

● Up to 1000 grey and common seals can be seen off Tentsmuir Beach, Newport on Tay, near St Andrews. Other Scottish seal resorts include Loch Linnhe (boat trips from Fort William), the Isle of Skye, Shetland, Orkney and several places along the Cape Wrath to John O'Groats road.

● One of the largest colonies is on the Isle of May in the Firth of Forth.

● Strumble Head in Pembrokeshire offers views of grey seals and pups.

Grey seals can dive deep and for surprisingly long periods. Their behaviour underwater has been studied in recent years in order to learn more about how to control damage caused by seals to fishing nets and salmon cages.

The chough

Although scarce and found only in the rugged west country, this sleek and sociable member of the crow family is responding to conservation efforts and its numbers are beginning to increase.

A bird of mountain, crag and sea-cliff, the chough – pronounced 'chuff' – has a soaring, wheeling flight. It is easy to recognise by its glossy black plumage, which contrasts with its bright red bill and legs. The chough is a bold and engaging character that seems to delight in showing off its aerial skills, indulging in flamboyant acrobatics and tumbling and diving at breakneck speed. This notion of showing off is confirmed by the chough's joyful call – a loud, yelping '*cheee-ow*' or '*kyaa*'.

Shrinking habitat
Once a common species of coastlines around the British Isles, the chough is now by far the rarest of Britain's breeding crows. It has been found in fewer

A chough is of a similar size to a jackdaw, but can be distinguished in flight by the upturned tips to its broad, rounded wings.

locations across Europe in recent years, too, and in many places the decline continues. This is mainly due to the reduction in traditional pastoral farming, with rough, unimproved coastal grassland grazed by sheep and cattle becoming increasingly scarce.

Choughs prefer to live by the sea, near cliffs topped by close-cropped turf where they can forage for their insect food. As the habitat diminishes in size, the insects that feed upon the grazing animals' dung become less abundant and therefore the choughs that feed on these insects also suffer. Insecticides used by farmers to control fly parasites in livestock have also had a detrimental effect by killing off insects in the animals' dung. The spread of bracken and the loss of rabbits through myxomatosis have also had a damaging effect.

One of the saddest losses was from the cliffs of Cornwall. The species was once so numerous there that it was known as the

Cornish chough and adopted as the symbol of the county, even appearing on its coat of arms. An attempt to reintroduce choughs bred in captivity was abandoned in 2001 because of foot-and-mouth disease, but later in the same year wild choughs started to arrive in Cornwall of their own volition, probably from France. This may have been as a result of efforts made by various conservation

The chough is protected under the Wildlife and Countryside Act 1981 Schedule 1. This affords the species the very highest level of protection, with special penalties for disturbance at the nest.

CHOUGH FACT FILE

A handsome and graceful bird, the chough is easily recognised by its long, red, down-curved bill and red legs. In flight it is the most acrobatic of all the corvids, wheeling and diving around coastal cliffs, its explosive cries echoing round the rocks.

● **NAMES**
Common names: chough, red-billed chough
Scientific name: *Pyrrhocorax pyrrhocorax*

● **HABITAT**
Mainly on and around coastal cliffs; sometimes rocky inland crags

● **DISTRIBUTION**
West Wales, Isle of Man, Islay and surrounding islands; all round Irish coasts except for east; a few in Cornwall

● **STATUS**
Range contracted throughout British Isles, but numbers show increase in Scotland; a total of about 1100 pairs, most in Ireland

● **SIZE**
Length 40cm (16in); weight 300g (11oz)

● **KEY FEATURES**
A glossy black bird with red legs and bill; wings long with prominent primary 'fingers'; juveniles duller, with orange-yellow bill

● **HABITS**
Skilful and playful in flight; gregarious even in breeding season; forms small flocks

● **VOICE**
Loudly vocal throughout year; a loud, ringing 'cheee-ow' or 'kyaa'

● **FOOD**
Ants, insect larvae and other soil-borne invertebrates; grain and berries in winter

● **BREEDING**
Eggs laid from early April to mid-May; usually one clutch; young fledge into mid-August

● **NEST**
A bulky, untidy structure of twigs and roots, bound with mud and lined with sheep's wool; sited in crevice in cliff or on ledge in cave, mine shaft or even building

● **EGGS**
Lays 3–5 pale buff, cream or green eggs, variably marked with brown or grey; incubated for 17–18 days

● **YOUNG**
Chicks fledge at around 38 days; remain with parents in family groups

The chough lays its creamy coloured, finely speckled eggs in a nest lined with wool and animal hair. Each pair produces one clutch per season, although two broods have occasionally been recorded in Ireland.

The adult's bill is curved and strikingly red.

The glossy black plumage has a blue and purple iridescence.

Distribution map key

▨ Present all year round

☐ Not present

Sturdy bright red legs and feet have strong black claws for gripping hold of rocks.

---

organistions to improve grazed farmland and encourage good ant populations. Seven birds were sighted in the county and a pair bred, raising four chicks. Young were also raised in 2003 and 2004.

Today the chough is found in a few coastal areas around the British Isles and is showing some signs of recovery. More than 800 pairs nest in Ireland, and in Wales there are just under 200 breeding pairs. Up to 60 or so pairs breed on the Isle of Man. In Scotland, where there are fewer than 70 pairs, the island of Islay has been their stronghold for around 100 years. These figures may be low, but they are still an improvement on those of a decade or so ago.

Flock behaviour

As with many other birds that live in groups, each chough recognises its fellow flock members and has a complicated relationship with them. Breeding pairs remain together throughout the year and can often be seen flying close to one another as the group travels around.

A definite pecking order exists within every flock, which allows the birds to live together harmoniously.

The chough's bill is ideally suited to probing for ants, worms, dung beetles and other insects found in closely grazed turf. The birds concentrate on areas where the sun's warmth stirs these creatures into action.

Looping flight

Choughs often indulge in sweeping dives and tumbling rolls, their splayed-fingered wings harnessing the wind with effortless ease as they fly in the gusting updraughts of coastal cliffs. Few other big birds can make such tight turns or manoeuvres, and a flock of choughs on the wing is a wonderful sight for any birdwatcher.

After accelerating upwards, the chough executes a tight turn, moving forwards while skidding sideways.

After flying crosswind, the bird stalls then plunges downwards, beating its strong wings to accelerate.

The bird uses the gust of wind and its own momentum to gain height.

Twisting its broad, blunt tail, the bird turns into the wind.

With a swoop, the chough glides in a leisurely fashion.

The chough soars effortlessly on the wind.

The chough will often give its loud, ringing call from a perch to advertise its presence. At such times, the bird will usually preen and flick its wings and tail to emphasise its display.

They exploit available food supplies without wasting time and energy on unnecessary disputes.

In their first two or three years with the group, young birds rise gradually up the ranks. This 'social climb' comes about through aggressive interactions, but birds rarely injure one another, because subordinate birds usually give way to more dominant individuals.

Prey such as ants and beetles often occur at high densities in small patches, but when there is a restricted supply, dominant birds will obtain sufficient food for their survival, even if it is at the expense of subordinate birds. This ensures that the high status members of the flock survive to carry the genes of the group into future generations.

Protective pair

Throughout the breeding season, a pair of choughs will chase away intruders that they perceive to be threatening their nest site. This applies to other choughs as well as to some crows, which may well view the eggs or young as a tasty meal. Ravens and carrion crows are always chased away, but jackdaws are sometimes allowed to approach quite closely.

One of the chough's most spectacular flying displays is performed when a peregrine falcon comes too close to the flock for comfort, especially if there are chicks present. Anyone lucky enough to be watching is then treated to the spectacle of two of the most acrobatic birds confronting each other in the air. The fleet and agile chough usually remains unharmed.

CHOUGH CALENDAR

JANUARY • FEBRUARY

Although the depths of winter can be a testing time for choughs, the mild temperatures experienced on the western coast of Britain usually keep snow from covering their feeding grounds.

MARCH • JUNE

Breeding pairs usually nest in their own territory, but some choughs form loose colonies. Egg laying reaches a peak from mid to late April and the chicks hatch just under three weeks later.

JULY • OCTOBER

The fledglings are assiduously cared for by their parents and return to roost at the nest site for several weeks. In September, family bonds loosen. Some young may join the local flock.

NOVEMBER • DECEMBER

As winter takes its toll, choughs congregate in large numbers at good feeding grounds. If their breeding territories are too exposed, the birds may have to leave and join a communal roost.

WILDLIFE WATCH

Where can I see choughs?

● The few areas where choughs breed are the best places to look for them. Coastal cliffs in Wales, the Isle of Man, Islay and surrounding islands in Scotland and the west of Ireland are chough haunts. The Isle of Man is particularly good for watching these birds. Use the cliff roads for spectacular views and take binoculars.

● These birds are not shy, but they will be upset if humans venture too close – so be considerate. For instance, watch choughs feeding on an area of cliff-top turf from a distance. If disturbed, the birds may move to a different area where ants and other invertebrate food are not so easy to find.

● Do not expect to spot a chough's nest. These are usually exceptionally well concealed in inaccessible places, such as in a cave down at sea level, on a rocky cliff or in an old mine shaft. Watch the comings and goings of the parent birds attending their offspring in the nest.

● When trying to spot choughs, take a close look at all the passing crows. Choughs are easily confused with jackdaws at a distance and the flight call is often the best clue to identity. Although there may be more jackdaws in an area than choughs, birds seen feeding on an area of short turf are most likely to be choughs.

Hidden nest

Chough nests are untidy structures of twigs and mud, lined with sheep's wool, and are difficult to see because they are usually sited high up at the back of a cave or in a mine shaft. However, intrepid birdwatchers and wildlife photographers have set up hides and meticulously recorded what goes on. The female chough begins incubation as soon as the first egg is laid. She lays between three and five eggs and relies on her mate to bring her food, although on occasions she will leave the nest to feed with the local flock some distance away.

When the chicks hatch after 17 or 18 days, the female broods them for ten days or more, feeding them morsels passed to her by the male in response to her begging. When the nestlings are between five and seven days old, the male will also feed them directly. Once they have fledged, at around 38 days old, the youngsters wait in individual hiding

places, emerging to compete loudly for food whenever their parents appear. After a week or so, the young birds move around in the open with the adults and learn how to forage for themselves.

A month later, the youngsters are feeding independently, but the family bond remains intact and may last throughout the winter and into the next breeding season. There are several records of 'helpers' at the nest, and one such bird was proved, by

means of colour ringing, to be one of the offspring of the breeding pair from the previous year.

This may seem a waste of the young bird's energy, but it makes good sense. When a young bird has no mate or territory of its own in which to breed, the next best thing is to help its parents rear more siblings. This provides the youngster with valuable experience in raising a family and puts it in a good position to inherit the territory should its parents later relinquish ownership.

Choughs are lively and sociable birds, most often seen in pairs or small flocks, although larger groups of birds sometimes build up. The relationship between breeding pairs of adults is long lasting.

The dunlin

A flock of dunlins performing synchronised aerobatics over a wide estuary or running along the shiny wet sands at low tide is an arresting spectacle. From a distance, the birds in flight could be mistaken for a windswept plume of smoke.

Dunlins congregate on seashores and mudflats almost all year round. In June and July, there may be only a few non-breeding birds, but by August numbers have started to build up and by autumn there are thousands. Estuaries are by far the richest feeding areas for these waders and have been likened to motorway service stations for birds, with different populations coming and going at different times and staying for varying periods. Many estuaries, such as the Wash in East Anglia and Morecambe Bay in Lancashire, are now recognised as internationally important sites for dunlins and other waders.

While flocks of dunlins feed voraciously on mudflats in autumn and winter, their nesting territories are usually located on the short, sparse vegetation of moorland dotted with peaty pools. The birds form loose colonies and the density of nests depends on the quality of the site. In the Uist islands off Western Scotland, for example, on the fertile, flower-rich grassland known as machair, there may be up to 30 pairs per square kilometre (about a third of a square mile), with some nests less than 10m (30ft) apart. More typical densities – from 1 to 3 pairs up to 10 or 11 pairs per square kilometre – occur on the Flow Country peatlands of the north-east Highlands.

In summer these landscapes are alive with breeding birds. Having arrived in late April, mature dunlins take over the territories they vacated the previous July. Surviving pairs tend to reunite, and some pairs have been known to return to the same site four or five years in a row. If one bird in a pair has not survived, or is more than a few days late, it will be replaced, usually by a younger unpaired bird now ready to breed in its second year.

Marking territory

Soon after arriving at the breeding ground, the male dunlin performs a beautiful display flight over his chosen territory. Climbing steeply, he hovers against the wind, then switches back, alternately fluttering and gliding, until eventually drifting down with his wings held in a distinctive 'V'.

DID YOU KNOW?

Many birds cough up pellets comprising the indigestible parts of their food. These hard fragments can be analysed to give an idea of the birds' diets. In the Arctic, dunlin pellets have been found to contain the tiny bones and teeth of lemmings. It is thought that the birds scavenge these fragments from carcasses abandoned by Arctic foxes, absorb some of the calcium to help with egg laying, then regurgitate the rest.

At low tide, dunlins spread out across the shore but as the tide comes in, the birds retreat and start to crowd together. Large numbers of birds gathered on the shore are likely to be dunlins as these are Britain's most abundant coastal waders.

DUNLIN FACT FILE

Britain's most common wader, the dunlin is a small, round-shouldered bird, with a dumpy body, medium-length legs and a slightly down-curved, longish bill. In autumn and winter, large gatherings can be seen on many estuaries, probing the soft mud for food.

● NAMES
Common name: dunlin
Scientific name: *Calidris alpina*

● HABITAT
Estuaries, mudflats, coastal pools and shallow water inland; summer breeding grounds are wet upland moors, especially in northern Scotland; some on salt marshes and damp grasslands near coast

● DISTRIBUTION
Breeds in uplands of England and Wales and in western Ireland, but largest populations nest in Scotland; also a passage migrant and winter visitor to many coasts and estuaries

● STATUS
About 9500 breeding pairs in Britain and 150 in Ireland; more than 700,000 individuals in winter

● SIZE
Length 16–20cm (6–8in); weight 40–50g (1½oz)

● KEY FEATURES
In autumn and winter, upper parts and upper breast brownish grey and rest of underparts white, white wingbar and dark streak on white rump; medium-length black legs; juvenile has rufous brown, scaly back and streaked flanks. In summer, adult has mainly reddish brown upper parts, a black-streaked breast and white belly with two large black patches. The black bill is almost straight or lightly down-curved

● HABITS
Gathers in large flocks outside breeding season; adopts hunched, head-down posture when feeding on open mud or in shallow water

● VOICE
Usual flight call is rough raspy, wheezing *'treep'*; display song is a piping trill

● FOOD
Insects, molluscs, crustaceans and worms

● BREEDING
Birds return to breeding grounds in March and April, and start to display and lay eggs in May

● NEST
Hollow in ground or in tussock under cover of low vegetation; lined with grass or leaves

● EGGS
Usually 4 eggs with brown blotches, streaks and spots; 1 brood, rarely 2

● YOUNG
Hatch in 21–22 days; quickly able to run around and feed themselves; fly and become independent at about 20 days

The dunlin's eggs are laid in a neat cup of vegetation in a scrape in the ground. Their colour and markings are variable, but they are usually well camouflaged to escape detection by predators.

In breeding plumage, the back is chestnut streaked with black.

The hind belly and undertail are white.

The black bill is almost straight or slightly curved downwards.

In summer, the dunlin has a black belly patch.

The black legs are of medium length.

Distribution map key

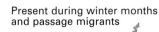

Present all year round

Present during breeding season

Present during winter months and passage migrants

Not present

◄ An incubating male dunlin blends in well with his surroundings even where vegetation is short. Camouflage is especially important to ground-nesting birds because they are potentially sitting targets for gulls and birds of prey.

► Unless they move, newly hatched dunlin chicks are extremely hard to spot. Their marbled and mottled brown and grey plumage breaks up their outlines most effectively.

◄ In summer russet plumage, a dunlin draws attention to itself only when displaying to attract a mate. Otherwise, it merges well with the vegetation and is easily overlooked.

All the while, he makes a trilling call, which carries across the bleak landscape.

The dunlin's nest is made from grasses and leaves, and built in a scrape on the ground or on a small tussock, concealed by vegetation. The well-camouflaged eggs are usually incubated by the male during the day and the female at night. Downy chicks hatch after three weeks and are soon able to walk and feed themselves.

Bustling activity

It is unusual to see just one dunlin foraging on the seashore; there are likely to be hundreds or even thousands, because the birds form large flocks in autumn and winter. They are so focused on feeding that they rarely glance up. The dunlin's feeding technique involves a rapid, mechanical series of pecks at the surface as the bird moves steadily forwards, leaving a distinctive trail of dots.

At first, the chicks are cared for and brooded by both parents, but the female often abandons them before they reach full independence. The male leaves soon afterwards, and by July all dunlins have usually departed from their moorland home and headed south to the coast.

Plover's protection
Different species of wader usually ignore each other, especially on their breeding grounds, but the dunlin has developed a special relationship with the golden plover, which breeds in similar locations. The reason for this may stem from the different feeding techniques of the two species. The golden plover runs with its head held high, then pauses and bends quickly to pluck food from the ground. With its upright posture, it is able to keep a constant lookout for possible danger.

Depending on what food is available and the state of the tide, dunlins sometimes simply pick visible items from the surface of the mud.

The dunlin, on the other hand, scurries around with its head held low as it probes the soft soil for food. Watching for danger is more difficult with this feeding strategy, so foraging dunlins often accompany golden plovers to take advantage of the early warning signals that the larger and more alert plovers provide.

Plovers are not always pleased with this attention and they sometimes attempt to drive their companions away. The dunlins stubbornly return, however, and if both species are to feed effectively, an uneasy truce must be established. Researchers have observed that dunlins feed more efficiently when 'protected' by golden plovers, while the plovers' feeding efficiency is barely reduced. In Orkney and Shetland, this habit of following golden plovers earned the dunlin the charming local name, 'plover's page'.

Dunlin on the move

There are several subspecies of dunlin in Europe, three of which are seen in the British Isles. The resident breeding dunlin, *Calidris alpina schinzii*, also breeds in south-eastern Greenland, Iceland and Norway, and spends the winter in Africa.

C. a. arctica breeds in north-eastern Greenland and winters in north-western Africa. These Greenland birds pass through the British Isles on migration. Birds that stop off on their way to and from summer and winter homes are known as passage migrants. The third subspecies, *C. a. alpina*, nests in northern Scandinavia, north-eastern Europe and Russia, and winters in India, north-eastern Africa, or in Britain and Ireland.

By far the majority of dunlins that overwinter around British and Irish coasts are not local breeders but *alpina* dunlin,

▲ In autumn and winter, at high tide, dunlins often gather on the shore, landing together after whirling in perfect synchrony, alternately flashing the darker and lighter underparts of their winter plumage.

although a few natives do spend the winter in areas such as the Severn Estuary. As migrants depart for Africa, so they are replaced by dunlin arriving from north-eastern Europe. These birds will moult and stay until spring. Only during peak times in autumn and early spring are representatives of all three subspecies found on the British coast together.

Once a dunlin reaches an estuary, its life is ruled by a new daily cycle, dominated by high and low tide rather than day and night. Food is available only at low tide, which occurs both at night and during the day. This means that

With the rising tide, dunlins use their bills to probe the mud, feeling for prey that is hidden from view.

If an individual dunlin finds a particularly rich area of food, its success is soon noticed by other birds and small groups gather.

As the sea comes in, the birds run about the shore, trying to find as much food as possible before the mudflats are covered and the water is too deep.

DUNLIN CALENDAR

JANUARY ● FEBRUARY

In winter, dunlin flocks gather on coastal mudflats. Major estuaries attract thousands of birds, which feed out on the wet mud at low tide and gather into tight groups on the shoreline at high tide.

MARCH ● APRIL

Dunlins moult into breeding plumage in spring. Southern migrants rest on British estuaries *en route* to the Arctic. Native birds return to their breeding territories on moors and marshes and start to display.

MAY ● JUNE

Once breeding pairs have been reunited, egg laying reaches a peak in May. The nesting birds are well camouflaged on their concealed nests. The young birds are up and about soon after hatching.

JULY ● AUGUST

Females are first to leave the breeding grounds and return to the estuaries to feed. Males and young birds are swift to follow. On the coast British birds are soon swamped by migrants from further north.

SEPTEMBER ● OCTOBER

The numbers of juvenile dunlins around the coast and on estuaries increase, as more migrants from Greenland and Russia arrive. British birds start to migrate south to their African wintering grounds.

NOVEMBER ● DECEMBER

Native dunlins are replaced by birds from northern Scandinavia and Russia. Large flocks may be seen feeding in the wet mud or wheeling and turning in the sky above their high-tide roosts.

dunlins often have to feed after dark in order to get at the rich reserves of worms and molluscs hidden in the mud.

Once the feeding grounds have been submerged, the birds form what is called a 'high-tide roost', assembling on sand or shingle spits, the shoreline or even on nearby farmland. These roosts are restless places, where tightly packed birds barge and push one another – particularly when dunlins from different subspecies are present. Nonetheless, they conserve vital energy by not flying and keeping movement to a minimum.

Autumn aerobatics

As the high-tide roosts form and disband, some of the dunlin's most dramatic aerial manoeuvres can be seen. Flocks of hundreds and sometimes tens of thousands of birds fly in tight formation. As the flock rapidly

changes direction, each bird within it banks and turns simultaneously. Alternately, grey backs and white bellies catch the light, which makes a startling spectacle. Such behaviour helps to attract other dunlins to join the roost for safety's sake – both peregrine falcons and merlins hunt lone waders in winter.

As winter comes to an end, migrant dunlin complete their moult and take on the plumage that will camouflage them on their moorland nesting grounds. Recently moulted British birds, arriving from Africa, fly to their breeding grounds, often stopping to feed on the estuaries first. Dunlins under one year old also head for the hills where they hatched. They may defend territories, but as they are not yet mature they will not mate for another year.

Dunlins make their homes on windswept estuaries and misty moorlands but numbers have declined in recent

A dunlin needs to feed almost constantly in the available time to survive. It usually preys on tiny creatures, but is quite capable of tackling a sizeable marine worm like this, which makes a nutritious meal.

◀ **Feather care is extremely important for the dunlin, as it is for all birds. Roosting dunlins spend much of their time preening, cleaning feathers, adjusting their alignment and removing dirt and parasites.**

▲ **When stretching its wings, a dunlin reveals the white wingbar that is otherwise seen only in flight. Most of the wing and mantle feathers of autumn dunlins are beautifully defined with pale margins.**

years. Taking steps to protect these birds will help to safeguard these last true wildernesses in the British Isles for future generations.

Food and warmth

Dunlins feed by sight and touch. They pluck tiny *hydrobia* snails from the surface and deeply probe the mud to feel for other quarry, such as crustaceans and worms, with their sensitive bill tips. The birds look like little animated sewing machines as they feed, using rapid in-and-out 'stitching' movements with their heads down and backs hunched as they work their way across the estuary. It appears that dunlins sift through the mud more thoroughly after dark, probably because at this time they are relying more on touch than on sight to find prey.

Dunlins weigh more in winter than at other times of the year, which is probably a form of insurance – either against food

shortages or, more likely, against gales and low temperatures. Estuaries in midwinter can be bitterly cold and small birds such as dunlins must eat enough food to build up a good layer of fat. This protects them from the cold and provides them with enough energy to survive high tides, when food is not readily available.

To prevent heat loss dunlins frequently stand on one leg while keeping the other tucked up in their feathers. They will even take off and land on one leg. In very cold weather, the birds fly with their legs and feet drawn forward into their belly feathers instead of trailing behind, which means they take on a different shape in flight.

Dunlins are among the first estuary waders to begin feeding and among the last to stop. Relentlessly, the birds follow the tide as it ebbs and flows, often feeding right at the edge of the water.

WILDLIFE WATCH

Where can I see dunlins?

● Look for dunlins on their coastal feeding grounds in autumn and winter. Almost any coast with mudflats is likely to attract a few dunlins, and high tide is the best time to see them when they are forced to move farther up the beach. Take care not to disturb roosting flocks, however, especially during cold weather, when the birds need to conserve energy.

● There are a number of RSPB coastal reserves where dunlins can be seen, sometimes in large numbers. These include Culbin Sands in north-east Scotland, Marshside and Morecambe Bay in Lancashire, Gayton Sands on the Dee Estuary in Cheshire, Snettisham and Titchwell in Norfolk, Langstone Harbour in Hampshire, the Hayle Estuary in Cornwall, Ynyshir in Cardiganshire and Belfast Lough in Northern Ireland.

● Reservoirs, such as Rutland Water in Leicestershire, and inland lakes or gravel pits with muddy edges attract dunlins in spring and late summer.

● Many of the places where dunlins breed are difficult to reach and observe without disturbing nesting birds. However, they can be watched safely at several RSPB reserves including Forsinard in north-east Scotland, Balranald on North Uist and Hoy in the Orkneys.

The fulmar

A true ocean traveller, the fulmar is more at home on the open sea than on land. A superb flier, it glides effortlessly over the waves and makes use of strong updraughts when flying around its cliff-face breeding colony.

Birdwatching from a ship can be fascinating. Hours, even days, can pass watching empty skies and yet suddenly – miles from land – birds appear. There are many oceanic species, but the one most likely to be seen anywhere in the North Atlantic at any time of year is the fulmar.

Fossil records of fulmar-like birds date back to the Lower Miocene period, 22 million years ago. Certainly, Vikings were familiar with fulmars and on the remote island of St Kilda, off the coast of Scotland, fulmar bones have been found together with artefacts from the 9th century. This group of Atlantic islands was the fulmar's only stronghold within the British Isles for centuries. Indeed, the St Kildan islanders relied on fulmars for at least a thousand years, not only for food, but also as fertiliser – they used the carcasses – and to provide oil, which was used both in lamps and medicinally. The first mention of a fulmar in the English language came in a book written in the late 17th century by Scottish traveller and writer Martin Martin, who worked for some time on St Kilda as a land steward.

It is thought that the first fulmars bred on mainland Iceland in the 9th century, and by 1900 they were so prolific that around 60,000 young birds were being taken for food each year. Fulmars are known to have reached the Faroe Islands by about 1839 and the Shetland island of Foula by 1878. Since then, the birds have colonised most parts of the British and Irish coasts, wherever there are suitable cliffs for nesting. The current annual breeding population is estimated to be well over half a million pairs.

A likely cause for the fulmar population explosion relates to the birds' liking for oily food. As the whaling industry became more important in northern waters, the stripping of whale blubber beside the boats provided the birds with a new and abundant food supply. Then, as whaling declined, so the fishing industry grew and again there was a by-product that benefited the scavenging fulmar – fish were gutted at sea and the waste material was thrown overboard.

This may not, however, be the whole story. Recently, experts have shown that the massive expansion in fulmar numbers is unlikely to have been based purely on breeding success. One theory suggests that a new genus arose in Iceland that was better adapted to breeding farther south, including Britain and Ireland, and in smaller colonies than those of the birds

SELF-DEFENCE

The fulmar has an unusual method of warding off predators. It stores oil from marine creatures and other foods in its stomach and can spit it out over a surprising distance, with impressive accuracy. This oil is truly foul-smelling and ornithologists report that the stench is so strong that clothes worn while catching fulmars for leg-ringing never lose their stink, even if they are buried in the ground. There seems little doubt that this unpleasant habit gave the species its old Icelandic and St Kildan name of *foul maa*, meaning foul gull.

The marine environment may seem harsh to us, but for a fully grown fulmar there are few predators. As a result, these birds are long-lived, and at least two individuals are known to have lived for well over 30 years.

FULMAR FACT FILE

These seabirds can be recognised by their flight – long glides with the wings held straight and firm, alternating with an occasional series of stiff, shallow wingbeats. On land, they appear rather clumsy and tend to squat on their lower legs.

● NAMES
English names: fulmar, northern fulmar
Scientific name: *Fulmarus glacialis*

● HABITAT
Open sea and coastal cliffs

● DISTRIBUTION
All round British coasts, wherever there are cliffs with suitable ledges for breeding

● STATUS
About 600,000 pairs breed in Britain and Ireland but the numbers may increase to 2 million individuals in winter

● SIZE
Length 45–50cm (18–20in); weight 700–900g (1lb 9oz–2lb)

● KEY FEATURES
Adult head, neck and underparts white; upperparts bluish grey; rump, tail and upperwings pale grey; dark eye; grey and yellowish bill strong and stubby with hooked tip and pronounced tubular nostrils; legs short, feet long and bluish green to pinkish; sexes alike

● HABITS
Seen in all weathers throughout the North Atlantic, spends much of its life far out to sea and may visit land only during nesting season; some individuals present at breeding sites in autumn and winter

● VOICE
Mostly silent at sea; pairing birds cackle loudly to each other

● FOOD
Crustaceans, fish, offal and carrion floating on sea, especially from trawlers

● BREEDING
Sites re-occupied from late autumn, but eggs not laid until May; young birds leave breeding colonies August–September; 1 brood per year

● NEST
No material on bare rock of cliff ledges; shallow depression in soft earth on clifftops, occasionally lined with small stones; sometimes on ground, sheltered by buildings or on buildings near coast

● EGGS
Single white egg, incubated for about 52 days

● YOUNG
Cared for by both parents; fledges at about 46 days, when it becomes independent

Distribution map key

Present all year round

Not present

The head is white with a dark smudge around the eye.

A thick 'bull' neck characterises the fulmar.

Narrow, pointed wings are bluish grey above and white beneath.

The tail is pale grey.

living in the high Arctic and North America. Today, there are seven species of fulmars. Six of them live in, or close to, Antarctica, while the northern fulmar is the only one to breed in the Northern Hemisphere.

Distinctive bill
Fulmars are often overlooked, because at first glance they appear very similar to the more familiar gulls. A closer look reveals that they differ from gulls in many ways,

however, and they are more closely related to albatrosses, shearwaters and petrels. Like albatrosses, fulmars belong to a group of birds called tubenoses. This name correctly describes the fulmar's bill, with its enlarged nostrils.

Enlarged tube-like nostrils give the fulmar a superb sense of smell. It can detect food and breeding colonies from great distances. The thick hooked bill is also typical of these birds.

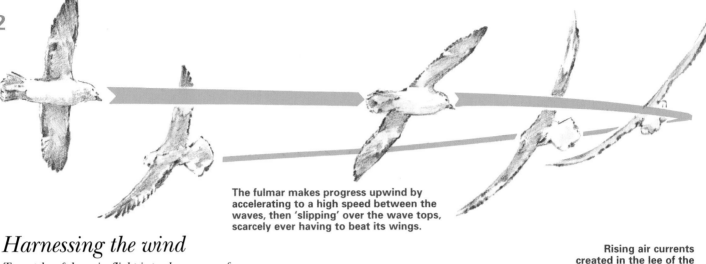

The fulmar makes progress upwind by accelerating to a high speed between the waves, then 'slipping' over the wave tops, scarcely ever having to beat its wings.

Harnessing the wind

To watch a fulmar in flight is to observe one of nature's evolutionary marvels. The bird glides on stiffly held wings – either low over the sea with its wing tips almost brushing the surface, or around its cliff-face colonies. Near the cliffs, it rides the air currents, executing amazing stalls, turns and changes of speed.

Rising air currents created in the lee of the waves enable it to glide for hours on end.

In the past, there have been various explanations for this curious adaptation, but scientists have now shown that it is associated with exceptional development of the part of the brain that detects smell.

Although fulmars are most often seen either singly or in pairs and lead what could be described as a nomadic lifestyle, they are also gregarious for much of the year. Flocks form where food is plentiful – for example, thousands of birds may gather to feed on a floating whale carcass.

Fulmars are also polymorphs, which means that they can have more than one plumage colour. There are two well-recognised extremes. One of these is dark – known as the 'blue phase' – and the other is pale. The pale fulmar is the type usually seen in Britain, while the blue phase is more numerous farther north. A whole gradation of intermediate colours occurs, as well.

A solitary egg

Fulmars are cliff-nesting birds and usually breed in colonies, the size of which varies from a few pairs to several hundred. No nesting material is used – the egg is simply laid on a narrow ledge. During population expansions, fulmars may use other sites, such as buildings, the soft soil at the tops of cliffs, or even patches of ground sheltered by stone walls.

The single egg is not usually laid until mid-May and most fulmar chicks do not hatch until early July. During this long incubation period of around 52 days, the female takes the first turn on the egg for

FULMAR CALENDAR

JANUARY ● APRIL

Most fulmars have returned to the previous year's nest sites or to the colonies where they were bred. In early spring, cackling fills the air as pairs prepare for breeding.

MAY ● JUNE

Most eggs are laid in May. The single egg rests on bare rock or in an earth scrape. Incubation is shared by both parents. Off-duty birds may travel many miles out to sea to feed.

JULY ● AUGUST

Newly hatched downy chicks are looked after by both parents for about seven weeks. Once fledged, they head out to sea and most will cross the Atlantic. Adults do not travel as far as juveniles.

SEPTEMBER ● DECEMBER

Immature fulmars spend several years out at sea off the coast of eastern Canada. Adults remain in European waters and by October, having undergone their annual moult, start to return to their colonies.

Once a pair of fulmars has bred successfully at a particular site, they are unlikely to change that site or, indeed, their mate. Before egg-laying begins, the pair leave the colony to fatten up.

Both parent birds feed their single chick on regurgitated food and stomach oil. One adult remains with the youngster to protect it for the first two weeks of its life. After around 46 days, the chick is ready to leave.

Fulmars are highly territorial at the breeding site. Fighting is rare but any disputes that do break out are settled by wrestling – gripping the rival by the wing – or by spitting.

a day or two and then disappears for around seven days to feed, leaving the male to take over. Eventually, she returns and shares the incubation equally with her mate.

Once the young fulmar becomes independent, it spends the next few years almost exclusively at sea, often hundreds of miles from land. Most of these youngsters find their way to the north-western Atlantic and the rich fishing grounds off the coast of Newfoundland. They may return to their breeding

colonies after four or five years, but will not start breeding until they are at least six years old, and possibly not until they reach 12 years of age.

Fulmar colonies are seldom completely deserted. Adult fulmars moult between August and October and spend most of that time out at sea, but even then many juveniles or lone adults may return to the breeding colony. By December, most adults are once again back in the area, and may be seen patrolling the cliff faces on their characteristically stiff wings.

Courting couples

Fulmars begin to return to their breeding cliffs in autumn following extensive wanderings in the North Atlantic. However, they do not lay their eggs until May. These long-lived birds pair for life and couples court one another with much bobbing and bowing, and a loud cackling chorus.

The courting ritual begins with cackling to the sky, and is followed by tender bill jousting and nibbling.

The pair bond is renewed each season. This female sits under an overhang, while her partner remains on guard nearby.

Periodically, the male may pass food to the female, perhaps to display his potential paternal skills.

The mackerel

Built for swimming at speed, the mackerel is perfectly streamlined. Even its fins can be flattened against its smooth-scaled body. In recent years, a decline in mackerel numbers has led to the imposition of strict fishing quotas.

Sleek and quick as a flash, the mackerel has an intriguing life cycle, disappearing to deeper water in winter but favouring shallow water in the warmer summer months.

The mackerel is immediately identifiable, but is usually only ever seen on the wet fish counter, its beautiful colours often faded or altered. Even in these circumstances, it is obvious that this is an animal built for speed. It has a long, torpedo-shaped body that tapers to a markedly forked tail fin and pointed snout. Its two dorsal fins are widely separated and a series of small, retractable, aerofoil finlets are located at the rear along its back and beneath its body. Nothing disrupts the mackerel's smooth lines – all its fins can be folded back to lie flush with the body, including the pectoral and pelvic fins, which settle into gentle depressions. Even the bulge of

the eye is covered by a smooth, gelatinous layer, and the scales are small, fine and silky smooth.

Muscular tail

Anatomically speaking, the mackerel is practically all tail. Its pelvic girdle is almost in line with its pectoral girdle, just behind the head, which is equivalent to a human's hips being immediately beneath the shoulders. All the mackerel's vital organs – its heart, stomach and reproductive organs – are at the front of its body. The trunk of the fish is solid muscle and tail bone. The secret of the

As with most other shoaling fish, mackerel bunch together tightly when danger threatens. This confuses all but the largest potential predators, such as dolphins – and, of course, humans – which actually exploit this behaviour.

mackerel's amazing turn of speed lies in this muscle, which also generates body heat, frequently keeping the fish at least 10 degrees warmer than the surrounding water temperature.

Unlike most other pelagic (ocean-living) fish, the mackerel does not have a swimbladder – the air sac that functions as a buoyancy aid in less active fish.

RESTING FISH

It was once believed that active fish such as mackerel never sleep. However, recent observations from submersibles and tethered cameras have shown that during their less active time of year, mackerel will occasionally cease swimming and lie in hollows on the sea bed for a while. While this whole area of research is in its infancy, it suggests that mackerel do not become unconscious as mammals do, but will switch off certain bodily functions, possibly including movement and digestion, allowing others to tick over, probably keeping a watchful eye open for potential predators.

MACKEREL FACT FILE

A member of the tunny family, the mackerel's long, slender profile reduces drag, while its striped back provides camouflage. Although the species is a prime target for both commercial and sport fishing, the largest individuals may be well over 30 years old.

● **NAMES**
English name: mackerel
Scientific name: *Scomber scombrus*

● **HABITAT**
Mid-water zones; deep waters in winter, shallower coastal waters in summer

● **DISTRIBUTION**
Found around all coasts of Britain and Ireland

● **STATUS**
Declining; under great pressure from fishing fleets

● **SIZE**
Length usually up to about 35–40cm (14–16in), largest recorded 70cm (2ft 4in); weight 1.2kg (2lb 10oz) on average, largest recorded 2.5kg (5lb 8oz)

MACKEREL AND THE LAW

In order to prevent overfishing and stock depletion, quotas for mackerel (and several other fish) are set by the EU. Fishing restrictions have been imposed off the south-west coast of Britain and parts of the North Sea to protect over-wintering populations of juvenile mackerel.

● **KEY FEATURES**
Iridescent blue-green with wavy blackish stripes on upper side, silvery underside; two well-separated dorsal fins with row of aerofoil finlets behind dorsal and anal fins

● **HABITS**
Migrate from spawning areas offshore to shallow waters to feed

● **FOOD**
Mainly plankton but also eats fish eggs and small fish

● **BREEDING**
Shoal in spring to spawn in natal waters on continental slope; up to 500,000 eggs per female (up to 90,000 in a single spawning); eggs float near the surface and drift with the current; they hatch in 2–6 days

● **YOUNG**
Newly hatched larvae with yolk sac are just 4mm (⅛in) long; at 2–3 weeks, yolk sac is absorbed and larvae start feeding on small plankton. After 1 year, they are 20cm (8in) long; in 2 years, when they reach sexual maturity, 30cm (12in) long

The mackerel's eyes are deep-set in a special jelly-like surround, which reduces drag as prey is chased at speed. The proportionately large size of the eyes helps the fish to see well in poor light.

Distribution map key

	Present all year round

The tail fin is crescent-shaped

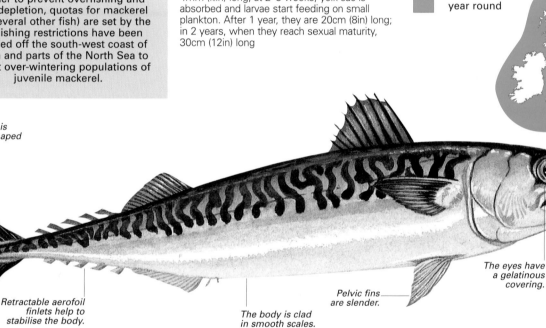

Retractable aerofoil finlets help to stabilise the body.

The body is clad in smooth scales.

Pelvic fins are slender.

The eyes have a gelatinous covering.

A swimbladder allows a fish to sense changes in pressure as it swims. The air sac expands and contracts to help equalise the pressure between the fish and its environment, in much the same way as people swallow or yawn to relieve pressure in their ears when flying. Mackerel, however, change depth at such speed, that a swimbladder would be a hindrance and could even rupture, killing the fish.

Distinctive body patterning identifies the mackerel. Its iridescent greenish or bluish ground colour is decorated with dark, wavy lines from front to back. These energetic fish are not easy to see, though, because they are almost always on the move and will try to avoid suspicious shapes approaching in the water.

Two centres

Two distinct populations of mackerel are found around British shores. One is based in the Celtic Sea to the south-west of Britain, but includes parts of Ireland's west coast, the Irish Sea, English Channel and western France. The other is found in the North Sea.

The highest concentrations of mackerel are found off the Norwegian coast, but as these are migratory fish there is likely to be an interchange between the two

When mackerel are tightly packed in response to the presence of a predator, the fish jostle for a position towards the middle of the shoal. Those on the outer margins of the shoal are more vulnerable to attack.

The mackerel's scales are exceptionally smooth and it slips through the water with ease. The silvery scales on the fish's flanks are also reflective at certain angles, so the fish can see each other even in near darkness.

The mackerel has countershading that camouflages it from predators in the open sea. The underside is silver, while the back is marked with black stripes or 'scribbles' on an iridescent blue-green background.

groups. The Celtic Sea mackerel move northwards around the western coast as far as the Shetland Islands and up the English Channel into the North Sea, while the North Sea fish migrate in all directions, including towards the Scottish and English coasts.

Prolific parents

The spawning period varies according to area. Fish in the Celtic Sea largely spawn in April and May, and those in the North Sea in June and July. The fish remain in deep water but move up to a depth of 150m (500ft). The Celtic Sea populations move offshore – away from the Cornish peninsula – to an area about 100km (60 miles) south-west of the Scilly Isles. The North Sea populations move inshore to spawn near the Norwegian coast.

Each female lays between a quarter and a half million eggs, in batches of up to 90,000 at a time. Each egg contains a large oil globule to aid buoyancy. The eggs rise up and float among plankton for about two days and are carried away from the spawning grounds by surface currents. Slowly, they sink to mid-water level where the larvae hatch after up to six days. Newly hatched larvae rely on their yolk sac for food and, when that is exhausted, they start to feed on small planktonic animals that proliferate in the surface layers of the sea. Once they reach a length of 13mm (½in) they start to resemble adults more closely. As they grow, they begin to tackle larger larvae and small fish.

The young mackerel grow rapidly at first, approaching 20cm (8in) in length by the end of their first year. The juveniles do not leave coastal waters until autumn and remain in the area between the spawning grounds and the shallower coastal waters for two or three years, when they begin to follow the older fish on their coastal migrations.

HORSE MACKEREL

The horse mackerel or scad (*Trachurus trachurus*) is a distant relative of the mackerel, and because it has similar habits and shares the same open water habitat, the two species are often grouped together. Although the horse mackerel bears a superficial resemblance to the mackerel, it is fatter in profile, its dorsal fins are closer together and it lacks the pattern of wavy lines down its sides and finlets at the rear of the body. It has a series of distinctive bony scales along its lateral line.

Young horse mackerel may be seen close inshore. The juvenile fish can sometimes be spotted sheltering among the tentacles of sea anemones, rather like the well-known clown fish of warmer waters. Horse mackerel may also be found among the tentacles of ocean-living jellyfish, despite the potential hazards.

The horse mackerel's streamlined profile and shoaling behaviour are typical of many medium-sized predatory fish.

During the summer, mackerel often move into inshore waters and spend much of their time hunting the fry of other fish, which favour the surface layers of the sea. This makes them an easy target for fishermen.

Avid feeders

After spawning, the migrating adult shoals, which have now been joined by juveniles born a year or two previously, make their way slowly to shallow waters nearer the coast. The mackerel are now feeding voraciously to make up for the energy expended during spawning. Unusually for a plankton-feeding fish, the foraging process is to a large extent selective, the fish eating only certain species. It is during this phase that mackerel are fished for and caught, mainly from boats.

Soon the fish break up into smaller shoals and begin taking larger prey, including young fish such as sprats and sand-eels, which are abundant in coastal waters at this time of year. The fact that mackerel tend to snap at anything that catches their eye makes them popular with fishermen in mid and late summer. Even a baitless but shiny bent pin will sometimes bring in a good-sized mackerel.

These inshore shoals are generally made up of sexually mature fish over 30cm (12in) long. The immature fish that were spawned the previous year tend to remain further offshore as they build up their bodies in preparation for breeding.

Autumn migration

During the latter part of the year, the adult shoals regroup and move offshore, where they increasingly favour the sea bed and feed on bottom-dwelling animals such as shrimps, worms and small fish. The mackerel form dense, localised concentrations distributed over a wide area. This phase lasts for about two months, generally from late December to February.

In late winter, the behaviour pattern changes once more. The mackerel begin nightly migrations towards the surface, following their planktonic food as it rises to the surface at dusk and sinks with daybreak, and the cycle begins again. In March, the Celtic Sea populations remain near the surface and prepare to spawn. In May, the North Sea group do the same.

Commercial fishing

Twenty-five or so years ago, mackerel landings at Cornish ports were in the region of 230,000 tonnes, but fishing on this scale was not sustainable. Instead of replacing itself, the mackerel population declined disastrously. Quotas were introduced and rigorously enforced in an attempt to halt the decline. Nonetheless, the large quantities of plump fresh mackerel familiar 25 years ago are less often seen today.

WILDLIFE WATCH

Where can I see shoals of mackerel?

● Mackerel are easiest to see in inshore waters between July and September. However, they will be at their most prolific at any given spot around the coast for just a few weeks. The precise timing varies from year to year according to the prevailing weather pattern.

● To see mackerel from the shore, watch from a rocky promontory that juts into the sea, using a pair of binoculars. The coasts of Devon, Cornwall and western Wales are probably the best places to choose. The fish are easiest to see on still days. During periods of particularly frenzied feeding, the shoals of fish will sometimes be drawn so close to the shore that they more or less brush the rocks with their bodies – astonishing behaviour for fish that generally favour open seas and oceanic waters.

● Garfish sometimes swim with a mackerel shoal. These can be recognised by their comparatively long, thin bodies, elongated pike-like heads and greenish coloration.

On warm, sunny days, when the water is calm, mackerel shoals are more likely to feed close to the surface as this is where their prey is likely to be concentrated.

Shrimps and prawns

Along the low-water mark on clean beaches, in creeks and estuaries, in eelgrass beds and in pools beneath cliffs on rocky shores, these crustaceans lurk unnoticed, their bodies changing colour to match their surroundings.

Common around most of Britain and Ireland, shrimps and prawns are wary creatures and remain hidden most of the time. When one does emerge from the shelter of a rock, it seems to be a mass of dangling legs and trailing whiskers – shrimps and prawns belong to the order Decapoda, meaning 'ten legs'. Far from being a nuisance when the animal swims among weeds or nestles in a crevice, these appendages represent a valuable array of tools and weapons and ensure both these crustaceans are extremely well adapted for life on or near the bottom of the sea.

Body armour

In common with other arthropods, shrimps and prawns have jointed limbs and segmented bodies with a protective outer covering, known as an exoskeleton. The shell covering the body and limbs grows from a rigid protein called chitin. The sections covering the joints are more flexible, although each hinge allows motion in one direction only.

As their bodies grow, shrimps and prawns must cast off their exoskeleton at intervals, then harden a new one as quickly as possible. The young invertebrates grow rapidly and may do this every fortnight, each moult taking

When feeding, the common prawn moves over the irregular sea bed on its last three pairs of legs, which have sharp ends that enable it to take dainty steps. The first and second pairs have small pincers for picking up edible debris.

IDENTITY CRISIS

No clear zoological distinction exists between the commonly used terms 'shrimp' and 'prawn'. Some say that the two names for these crustaceans are interchangeable, while others argue that prawns are larger. Prawns grow up to 10cm (4in) long, while shrimps are usually about 5cm (2in) but can reach 9cm. Most biologists agree, however, that animals belonging to the genera *Crangon, Philoceras* (and others) are shrimps, while those belonging to *Palaemon* and other genera such as *Pandalus* are prawns. One way to differentiate between them is to look at the 'snout' or 'beak' (called the rostrum). On the prawn it is long and curves upwards.

The body of the common shrimp changes colour, chameleon-style, to match the surface along which it is scuttling.

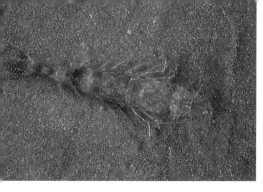

▲ Shrimps burrow into sand or seek shelter in empty shells during the day, emerging only at night to feed on small ragworms, tube-worms, molluscs and other crustaceans – including their own species.

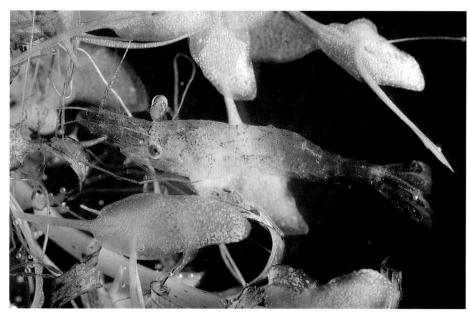

▶ The transparent body of a shrimp makes it hard to spot as it blends with its surroundings in a rock pool. Only the pigments in its eyes are noticeable.

no more than 20 seconds. The moulting process – known as 'ecdysis' – involves shedding the tough outer skeleton from the entire body, including the antennae, the transparent covering of the eyes and even the finest hairs, together with the first and last parts of the gut. Each time, a perfect copy of the body is left behind as the animal quickly retreats into a crevice while its body hardens sufficiently to protect it from predators once more.

Multiple attachments

The whiskers protruding from the head are either adapted as sensory organs, such as the two pairs of antennae, or used for feeding. Five pairs of whiskers are used to manipulate prey while a row of teeth on the rostrum – the upward curving tip of the shell between the eyes – enables the animal to chew.

Shrimps and prawns swim slowly by beating five pairs of flattened, paddle-like swimming limbs, called swimmerets, which are attached to the abdomen. To escape danger, they propel themselves backwards rapidly by bending and flexing the abdomen, and flapping their fan-shaped tail.

Between the antennae and the swimmerets are two pairs of swimming legs and then three pairs of walking legs. The swimming legs in the male differ slightly from those in the female, because the male must cling to his mate during copulation. The second pair have a so-called 'masculine appendage', used to help transfer his packet of sperm.

Mating occurs when the female is soft-bodied after moulting. The male shrimp turns the female on to her back and bends his body into an arc across hers, bringing their reproductive pores

In deep water, prawns often adopt a characteristic pink colour, which makes them practically invisible.

together. In prawns, the female is approached from behind by the male, who swings his abdomen to one side and underneath her body. In a few seconds they separate.

The eggs are shed within a couple of hours of mating. The female shrimp lies on her side when brooding eggs, whereas the female prawn remains upright with her walking legs splayed out.

Egg protection

Shrimps spawn in summer or winter while prawns spawn in the summer only. In the month before mating, the female assumes 'breeding dress' – special hairs grow on the swimming legs (pleopods) to hold the eggs. The fertilised eggs are crowded into the spaces between the pleopods

◀ Newly hatched larvae float in plankton, first using their front legs to swim, then slowly switching this function to their abdominal limbs as they go through a series of moults.

alongside her gills and carried for several months depending on the water temperature. Female shrimps may carry up to about 15,000 eggs, but prawns only up to 4000 or so.

Natural predators

Numbers of shrimps and prawns peak in the late summer and early autumn, swelled by the new generation. They are preyed upon by adult fish, such as cod, haddock and whiting. Birds also feed on them, particularly in shallow bays and estuaries, and seals scoop up large quantities in some areas. Humans are thought to take only a quarter of those lost to natural predators.

WILDLIFE WATCH

Where can I see shrimps and prawns?

● Choose a moderately sized rock pool with plenty of weed cover. You may see nothing at first, because these crustaceans react quickly to shadows, but after a few minutes they should emerge, antennae flicking in all directions as they search for food. Keep absolutely still as any movement will send them scuttling back under cover.

Common limpets

Clamped tight to rock faces to which they hold fast under the pounding of the stormiest of seas, limpets come to life when submerged at high tide. Then they glide a short distance to feed, leaving tracks in their wake.

Low tide is the time to look for common limpets (*Patella vulgata*). They often congregate in groups, covering large patches of rock, protected by their tough, conical shells. Each shell is slightly raised, leaving a tiny gap to allow in air, but if danger threatens, the animal will clamp its shell firmly to the rock face and no amount of prodding will dislodge it. Indeed, this is the origin of the phrase 'clinging like a limpet'.

Each limpet has its own favourite resting spot to which it always returns. On soft rocks, the scouring action of its shell erodes a circular depression as it rotates into position when clamping itself down. This scar in the rock matches the edges of the animal's shell exactly. A perfect fit is important to the limpet's survival because even the slightest gap will render it vulnerable to seabirds and other predators. Where the rocks are hard and cannot be worn down, the same effect is achieved by the erosion of the edge of the limpet's shell to match the surface irregularities.

The common limpet clings to the rock face using strong muscles in its sucker-like foot, which also secretes a sticky mucus. When the limpet is ready to move, it produces mucus that has a more fluid consistency, which helps to wash away the adhesive substance and creates a slippery surface on which the limpet can glide over the rocks.

Shore levels

Limpets that live at different levels of the beach have different shaped shells. Those living high on the shore are left exposed for longer than those lower down. Their shells are clamped to rocks for a greater part of the daily cycle and this extended pull on the sides of the shell produces a taller, more pointed shell than is seen in limpets living lower down the shore. Conversely, individuals that are permanently submerged have low, broad shells that are better able to resist the pounding action of the waves.

Common limpets are found at all levels, whether the shore is sheltered or exposed, but they are most abundant at mid-tide level. Their close relatives, china limpets (*Patella ulyssiponensis*), prefer low-tide levels but also live in mid-shore rock pools. The black-footed limpet (*Patella depressa*) is usually found at mid-tide level on exposed shores.

Feeding time

To avoid dehydration, limpets usually feed when the tide is in, especially those that inhabit level surfaces. However, during damp weather, those attached to steep slopes may be active at night even when the tide is out.

▲ Prised from its rock and viewed from below, this limpet reveals the sucker-like foot that clamps the animal to the rock. The tentacles and rasping mouth are also visible inside the shell.

◄ Where suitable resting spots are at a premium, limpets will gather in large colonies at every level of the rocky shore.

BLUE LIMPETS

The blue-rayed limpet is found all around the coasts of the British Isles on fronds of kelp at the low-tide mark. This limpet has a translucent shell shot with streaks of peacock blue. As it grows, it often migrates from the fronds to the stalk of the kelp, where it makes a deep scar as it lives out the last few months of its year-long life. These scars are instantly recognisable in kelp that has been cast up on the strand line during winter storms.

▲ The stunning colours of the blue-rayed limpet can only really be appreciated in living animals. The shells of washed up limpets are invariably dull and lacklustre in appearance.

Limpets start to move about 15 minutes after the tide has covered them. They travel at about 6cm (2½in) a minute, in a fairly straight line, to a chosen feeding ground that may be up to a metre (3ft) away but is usually within about 50cm (20in) of their resting places. There the limpets slow to less than one millimetre a minute as they graze on tiny plants.

The limpet scrapes young seaweeds off the rock by pushing out its rasping tongue, which is moved back and forth over a gristly pad. The head swings from

Each limpet erodes its own unique depression in the surface of the rock. Soft rocks may be pock-marked by the scars of previous incumbents.

▶ Limpets scrape algae from the surface of rocks using their rasping tongues or radulas. Their feeding tracks, easily seen at low tide, are especially evident on damp days.

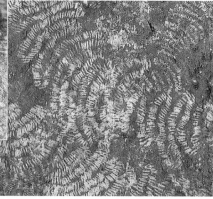

◀ When feeding, the limpet moves around on a muscular foot, in the same way as a garden snail. As it grazes, it pokes its head out from beneath its shell, revealing transparent tentacles.

side to side, leaving a characteristic zigzag pattern on the rock face. Each day the limpet grazes a different area of the rock. This gives the young plants a chance to regrow and ensures that the food supply is not exhausted.

Each limpet instinctively knows when the tide is due to turn, which enables it to judge when to return to base. It arrives back at its special spot just 15 minutes before the tide uncovers it again but how it does this is not entirely clear. It probably uses a combination of several methods, such as visual recognition of landmarks, setting a course by polarised light or sensing the prevailing flow of water. The limpet also makes use of the mucus trail that it left as it travelled over the rock on its outward journey.

Complex breeding

At first, common limpets have male characteristics, but some change to females at around the age of four as they mature. The overall ratio of males to females probably dictates how many individuals change sex and there may be an intermediate period when the limpet has both male and female organs at the same time.

Spawning takes place between October and December, possibly induced by rough seas that scatter the eggs some distance

▲ Feeding forays may take a limpet up to a metre from its resting spot, but it's always back before the rock is exposed.

away from the parents. Each fertilised egg turns into a larva, called a trochophore, which floats in the plankton for a few days before settling in a rock pool or some other permanently damp environment.

As it matures, it grows stronger and more able to cope with the heaving seas. The limpet finally moves to exposed rocks, taking up a position where it may live for between five and 16 years.

WILDLIFE WATCH

Where can I see limpets?

● The common limpet can be seen all around Britain and Ireland. The china limpet is found from the Isle of Wight along the south and west coasts right round Scotland and as far south as Grimsby. It is also found all around the coastline of Ireland. The black-footed limpet may be seen from Anglesey in North Wales, down around the west coast of Wales and England, and along the south coast as far as the Isle of Wight. It is absent from most coasts in Ireland.

Piddocks and shipworms

Using their shells as boring tools, these molluscs tunnel into soft rock or wood. A collection of perfectly round holes shows that piddocks are present, but shipworms leave only minute external clues.

A bivalve mollusc has two hinged shells that close protectively over the soft tissue within. Most have evolved for burrowing. Cockles, razorshells and tellins, for instance, pull themselves down into the sediment with a massive, muscular foot, and their shells provide a buttress against the sand. They are well protected against predators, and provided they can reach the water above, they are able to feed and breathe. However, some bivalves go a step further and bore into wood or even soft rock to hide.

Rock dwellers

Limestone, shale, clay and sandstone are all inhabited by stone-boring molluscs called piddocks, of which four species are to be found in Britain and Ireland – the common piddock (*Pholas dactylus*), the white piddock (*Barnea candida*), the wrinkled rock borer (*Hiatella arctica*) and the oval piddock (*Zirfaea crispata*).

These molluscs, which grow to between 4cm (1½in) and 9cm (3½in) long, have hard-edged shells with which they rasp away at the rock. The foot anchors the body and special muscles rotate the shell through 180 degrees. After this, they reverse to make the other half-turn, so that a cylindrical tunnel is bored into the rock. Most piddocks bore straight down but the white piddock, which bores into wood as well as rock, burrows horizontally.

Some piddocks, such as the wrinkled rock borer, remain on the surface if they find a suitable hole or crevice. They anchor themselves by means of secreted threads that act like strong guy ropes. The oval piddock, which is stubbier than the common piddock, is found mainly in clay and shale, and its dirty-looking white shells have a definite furrow.

When piddocks die, their boreholes may be occupied by other animals seeking sanctuary, such as brittlestars, sea cucumbers and small hairy crabs. However, the holes eventually weaken the rock and chunks break off and fall to the bottom of the gulley or pool.

Wood inhabitants

The shipworm is not a worm at all but a bivalve mollusc, although so modified that it is hard to recognise as such. It begins life as a planktonic larva, borne by ocean currents and feeding on tiny plants

▲ **The common piddock bores up to 15cm (6in) beneath the surface and extends a pair of siphons to the mouth of its burrow to feed and breathe.**

▼ **In some rocks, large numbers of boreholes show that numerous piddocks live in very close proximity. If one piddock runs into another, it is likely to bore straight through its neighbour.**

and animals. It gradually develops a miniature foot and two tiny shells. As the larva is able to detect lignin – a complex chemical that is a major component of wood – it can recognise timber when it comes into contact with it by chance. Once located, the larva attaches itself to the wood and its two shells rock against each other rather like an oil-well drill, using knob-like projections between the shells as a fulcrum. Before long, the movement wears a depression in the surface of the wood, which quickly

▲ A sucker foot protrudes through the permanent gape between the two halves of the piddock's shell. The piddock grips the sides of the hole with this foot, and rocks the shell from side to side, rasping away the walls.

► When a piddock is removed from its borehole, its siphons and foot can be seen projecting from the elongated shell. The excavated hole is so perfectly round that it might have been made by a power drill.

USING SIPHONS

As piddocks tunnel into the rock, they get rid of excavated material by drawing it into their bodies and expelling it through one of the two tubes they use to feed and breathe. These tubes, which are joined along their length and extend just out of the mouth of the burrow, act as siphons. Water is drawn in, food and oxygen extracted and the water is pumped out again, taking all waste material with it.

Males and females release their sperm and eggs directly into one of these tubes and thus into the water where the eggs are fertilised. The resulting larvae float in the plankton before developing into adult piddocks.

deepens as the shipworm's body elongates at a rate of about 2cm (¾in) a day. The sawdust that is shaved off is passed through the gut and digested. The tiny hole through which the shipworm enters the wood is left open as its connection to the water. The currents running into and out of its boreholes, which can be up to 60cm (2ft) long, bring in oxygen and planktonic food and take away the animal's waste.

The first depression is made in any direction in the wood, but as the borehole deepens, the shipworm turns to burrow along the line of the grain. The tunnel is lined with a chalky 'plaster' to make a secure internal wall – a device said to have inspired the Victorian engineer Isambard Kingdom Brunel in his design for a tunnel under the Thames. The

shipworm soon develops two more small shells at its rear end, which lock the animal to the burrow wall.

Riddled wood

The hole by which the larva first enters the wood remains barely noticeable but inside the wood the burrow widens out to about 1cm (⅓in). A ship's timber or a breakwater can appear unaffected from the outside, while being practically hollow inside and liable to collapse. This is precisely what happened to the wooden dykes in Holland in the early 18th century, resulting in near disaster for this

low-lying country. It was a Dutch zoologist who first identified the shipworm as a bivalve mollusc.

From time to time, a piece of mollusc-infested wood, broken off from a breakwater or pier pile, may be left temporarily high and dry. When this happens, the shipworm closes off the entrance to its bore with its body and the water trapped in the burrow will keep it alive for a few days. The shipworm also has the ability to generate its own oxygen from the high levels of carbohydrate in its tissues.

WILDLIFE WATCH

Where can I see piddocks and shipworms?

● Piddocks are best seen at low tide on sandstone or compacted clay shores. Parts of the Norfolk coast are good, but the most spectacular colonies can be found at Orcomber Point in Devon. Piddocks glow greenish blue at night.

● Shipworms, or their remains, can be found in almost any piece of sizeable driftwood washed up on the shore.

▲ Shipworms have caused problems for sailors and marine engineers for centuries. Timber used for boats and sea defences can be destroyed from the inside out by their burrows.

► Shipworms secrete a complex enzyme called cellulase, which enables them to eat wood by breaking down the cellulose. This takes many days, but releases about 80 per cent of the wood's nutrients.

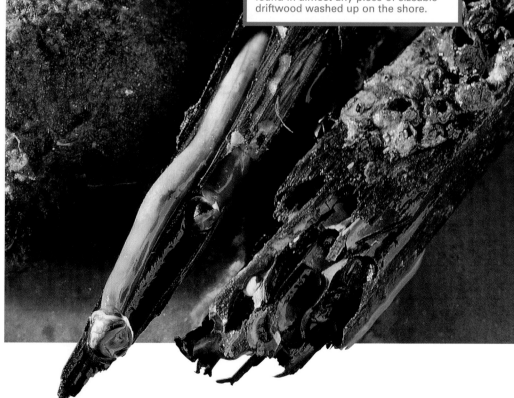

Sand hoppers

Swarms of these tiny creatures may be seen in constant motion along the strand line, their lives dictated by the ebb and flow of the tide. With their diet of rotting debris, they help to keep beaches clean.

Large numbers of small, scuttling creatures can be found along the shores of the British Isles, spending much of their lives hiding among rocks or seaweed. They include an important group of marine crustaceans called amphipods, the most numerous of which are the sand hoppers, or gammarids.

These tiny invertebrates will drown if submerged for too long and so they live among rotting seaweed, just above the tideline, and feed at night on the weed and organic debris washed up by the sea.

One jump ahead

Sand hoppers move up and down the shore as the tide ebbs and flows. They do not like to be fully submerged. Each sand hopper can jump up to 50 times its own body length, either into the air or along the ground, by flicking its abdomen and hindmost three pairs of legs. These giant leaps are not only a useful way of making a quick escape from the incoming tide or from predators, such as gulls, waders, rock pipits and other birds, but they also help sand hoppers to find new sources of food.

As the tide rises, the sand hoppers adjust the direction of their hopping so that they remain just ahead of the lapping waves. This may involve climbing cliffs or sea defences, and they may even enter houses built on the beach.

When the tide begins to fall again, the sand hoppers follow it down the shore, leaping along in search of scraps of food left behind by the receding waves. Eventually, they return to the sand, shingle or rocky reef, where they burrow or nestle into crevices.

▶ **Vulnerable to drying by the wind and sun, sand hoppers rarely venture far from the damp strand line.**

▼ **Sand hoppers have remarkable powers of navigation. They use the angle of the sun as a compass.**

Sand hoppers living on the eastern coast of Britain follow the falling tide by moving eastwards. Experiments have shown that if several individual sand hoppers are transported to a beach on the western coast and released as the tide recedes, they continue to move eastwards, even though this takes

Orchestia gammarella **is slightly smaller than its relative,** *Talitrus saltator,* **and is reddish or green-brown in colour. It can be recognised by the large claws on the third pair of legs.**

them away from the sea. Research such as this implies that these animals have a 'memory' relating to their home habitat.

Navigating by the sun

Sand hoppers use visual clues to their whereabouts, but they have a more sophisticated navigational system to ensure that they remain in the best position on the damp shore as the tide changes. If displaced up or down the shore, they will return to the zone on the beach from which they were taken, by using the angle of the sun as a guide. If a mirror is placed on the beach to reflect the sun's rays from a different direction, they can be fooled into moving the wrong way.

Since the sun moves continuously throughout the day, using it as a navigational aid depends on adjusting to this movement, which sand hoppers are able to do. When taken from their home beach to another shore at a different longitude, their movements

SPECIALISED DESIGN

Like shrimps and prawns, the sand hopper is an arthropod, so it has a hard outer skeleton, with jointed limbs that are designed for all kinds of different tasks – a bit like a Swiss army knife. These limbs are used to sense the animal's surroundings, to feed, walk, burrow, swim, clean its body and reproduce.

This tiny crustacean can grow only by casting off its old skeleton, increasing to a new size and hardening the outer surface again. It will do this many times during the first few months of its life, until it reaches maturity at about six months old. The sand hopper breeds in summer and the female broods several eggs in a pouch under her body.

Three species of sand hopper are commonly found in Britain and Ireland. *Talitrus saltator* may reach 2cm (¾in) long and occurs in vast numbers on sandy beaches. *Orchestia gammarella* frequents rocky or shingle shores. The less common *Talorchestia* inhabits both sandy and rocky shores – hence its name is a combination of the other two.

▲ **The sand hopper has a curved and laterally flattened body. It hops by using its abdomen and last three pairs of legs as a spring, and moves in the sand by wriggling along on its side.**

occur at the same time as they would have done if they had stayed at their original location.

Another curious trait is that on beaches where rocks and reefs jut out from the sand or pebbles, sand hoppers will always move towards the lowest point on the horizon. This means that they will find the gaps between the rocks and so avoid climbing obstacles as they move up and down the shore, thus saving vital energy.

Although sand hoppers are not true marine creatures, since they cannot live under water, their life cycle is bound up with the sea.

▶ *Talitrus saltator* **is brownish grey or green in colour with a curled rear end. It is common on sandy shores wherever seaweed accumulates and burrows in well-drained sand just above the high-tide mark.**

WILDLIFE WATCH

Where can I see sand hoppers?

● At any time of year, all around the British Isles wherever rotting seaweed piles up on the strand line, sand hoppers will be abundant. Simply turn over a stone or lift some weed and these tiny crustaceans will emerge, leaping frantically in all directions.

● The similar size, shape and habits of the two most common British species of sand hopper, *Talitrus saltator* and *Orchestia gammarella*, means they are not easily distinguished at a glance.

Sand hoppers emerge mainly at night to feed, when they are safer from shore birds, their main predators, than they are during the day. They try to jump to safety when disturbed and burrow back under cover.

Gentians and centauries

On sand dunes, shingle and coastal grassland, native gentians and centauries bloom on sunny days, their brightly coloured flowers arranged in branched clusters. Most of them have been used in herbal remedies for hundreds of years.

The delicate pink or purplish flowers of gentians and centauries are most often associated with high European mountains. While they are indeed widespread in such regions of the Northern Hemisphere, 17 species are native to Britain and Ireland. Most occur in the lowlands and several of them, such as autumn gentian and common centaury, are familiar, especially on limestone soils. Many grow around the coasts, although some prefer conditions inland. Gentians and centauries belong to the family Gentianaceae, which worldwide includes about 1200 species.

Some of the British plants are scarce and four of them – alpine, spring, fringed and dune gentian – are included in the Red Data Book of Britain's rarest plants. They are also listed under the Wildlife and Countryside Act Schedule 8, which protects them from being uprooted or even picked.

Dune gentian is becoming rare all over northern Europe, so the British colonies are important, while fringed gentian has grown at just one site, in the Chilterns, since 1982. Lesser and seaside centaury are included in the Irish Red Data Book, with the latter protected by law in Northern Ireland.

In Britain and Ireland, most gentians and centauries are annuals or biennials and die after flowering, often in late summer or autumn. Only three native species are perennial: marsh gentian spring gentian and perennial centaury. The latter two produce numerous, non-flowering shoots and short runners, and can form extensive, long-lived patches in grassy swards. Marsh gentian grows in areas of bog and wet heath in England and Wales, and is increasingly rare.

Few of the native plants display the famous gentian blue of those found in Alpine pastures, but their flowers are often an attractive purple, lilac or pink, while two species have bright yellow flowers. The leaves contain bitter chemicals called glucosides that deter grazing animals.

Tubular flowers
The petals form a tube, which is flared at the mouth into five – or occasionally four – spreading lobes. In the true gentians (from the genus *Gentiana*) the petal lobes have smaller lobes or pleats between them. In the group sometimes known as felworts (from the genus *Gentianella*), these are lacking or are replaced by a fringe of hairs. Five stamens, the male organ of the flower, are attached to the inside of the petal tube. After pollination and fertilisation, the ovary develops into a fruit known as a capsule, which splits when ripe to release tiny seeds.

▲ The purple blooms of field gentian can be seen in pastures and among coastal dunes, although the species is declining in Wales and central and southern England.

◄ The candy pink flowers of common centaury are borne in small clusters and usually close up in the afternoon.

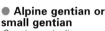

Marsh gentian
Gentiana pneumonanthe

GENTIAN FACT FILE

● **Marsh gentian**
Gentiana pneumonanthe
Habitat and distribution
Thin, peaty soils on damp heaths from
Dorset to Cumbria, and on Anglesey in
north Wales
Size 10–40cm (4–16in) tall
Key features
A perennial with slender, erect, leafy
stems; leaves spear-shaped, 1-veined;
flowers rich blue with greenish streaks,
bell-shaped, solitary or in clusters of
2–6, about 25mm (1in) long, 5 petal
lobes with smaller, pointed lobes
between them
Flowering time
July–October

● **Spring gentian**
Gentiana verna
Habitat and distribution
Short, rocky grassland on limestone in
Upper Teesdale; abundant in the Burren
and other districts around Galway Bay,
Co Clare in western Ireland
Size 5–17cm (2–6½in) tall
Key features
A low perennial with short runners and
numerous leafy rosettes; leaves
elliptical or spear-shaped, mostly basal
but 1–3 pairs along flowering stems;
flowers intense blue, solitary, about
22mm (1in) long, 5 petal lobes with
small, lobes between them
Flowering time
April–June

● **Alpine gentian or
small gentian**
Gentiana nivalis
Habitat and distribution
Rare on lime-rich mountain ledges and
vegetated scree above 700m (2300ft)
in two small areas of the central
Highlands of Scotland
Size 2–15cm (¾–6in) tall
Key features
A low, small, slender, often unbranched
annual; leaves mostly along the stems,
elliptical or oval; flowers intense blue,
solitary, about 10mm (½in) long,
distinctly longer than 5-angled calyx of
sepals surrounding them
Flowering time
July–August

The bell-shaped flowers of the
rare marsh gentian are a rich
purplish blue, with a green stripe
on the outside of each petal.

Spring gentian
Gentiana verna

The stunning blue flowers of spring
gentian are now a very rare sight.
True blue is an unusual colour in
nature and these are the most brilliant
blue of all wild flowers found growing
in the British Isles.

**Alpine gentian or
small gentian**
Gentiana nivalis

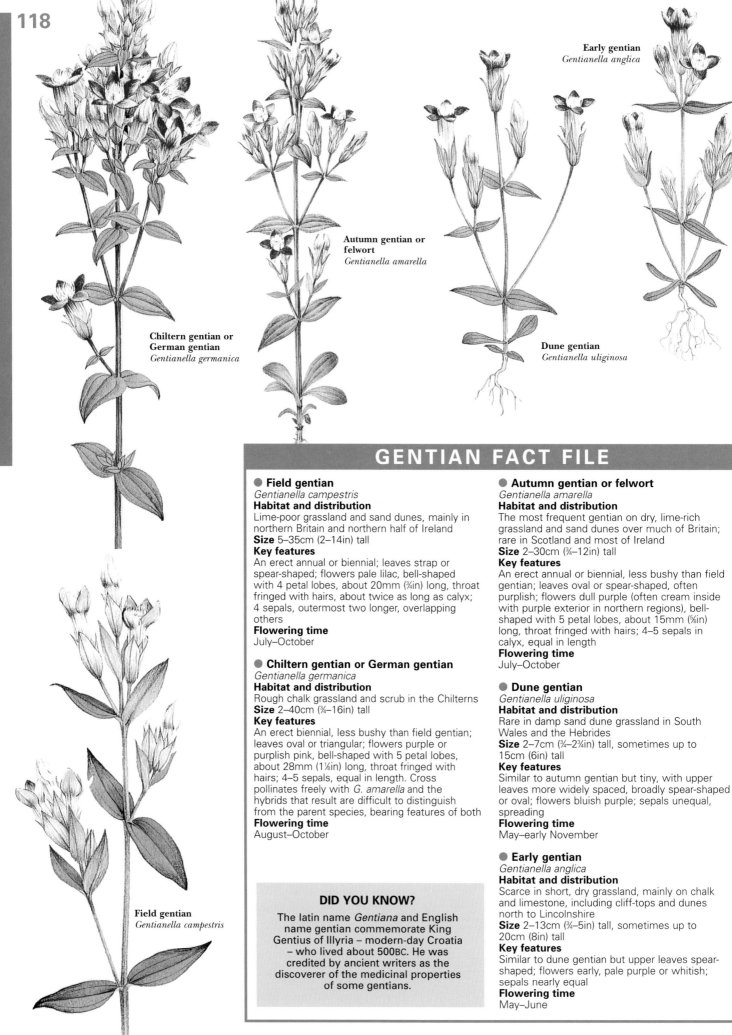

Early gentian
Gentianella anglica

Autumn gentian or felwort
Gentianella amarella

Chiltern gentian or German gentian
Gentianella germanica

Dune gentian
Gentianella uliginosa

Field gentian
Gentianella campestris

GENTIAN FACT FILE

● **Field gentian**
Gentianella campestris
Habitat and distribution
Lime-poor grassland and sand dunes, mainly in northern Britain and northern half of Ireland
Size 5–35cm (2–14in) tall
Key features
An erect annual or biennial; leaves strap or spear-shaped; flowers pale lilac, bell-shaped with 4 petal lobes, about 20mm (¾in) long, throat fringed with hairs, about twice as long as calyx; 4 sepals, outermost two longer, overlapping others
Flowering time
July–October

● **Chiltern gentian or German gentian**
Gentianella germanica
Habitat and distribution
Rough chalk grassland and scrub in the Chilterns
Size 2–40cm (¾–16in) tall
Key features
An erect biennial, less bushy than field gentian; leaves oval or triangular; flowers purple or purplish pink, bell-shaped with 5 petal lobes, about 28mm (1⅛in) long, throat fringed with hairs; 4–5 sepals, equal in length. Cross pollinates freely with *G. amarella* and the hybrids that result are difficult to distinguish from the parent species, bearing features of both
Flowering time
August–October

● **Autumn gentian or felwort**
Gentianella amarella
Habitat and distribution
The most frequent gentian on dry, lime-rich grassland and sand dunes over much of Britain; rare in Scotland and most of Ireland
Size 2–30cm (¾–12in) tall
Key features
An erect annual or biennial, less bushy than field gentian; leaves oval or spear-shaped, often purplish; flowers dull purple (often cream inside with purple exterior in northern regions), bell-shaped with 5 petal lobes, about 15mm (⅝in) long, throat fringed with hairs; 4–5 sepals in calyx, equal in length
Flowering time
July–October

● **Dune gentian**
Gentianella uliginosa
Habitat and distribution
Rare in damp sand dune grassland in South Wales and the Hebrides
Size 2–7cm (¾–2¾in) tall, sometimes up to 15cm (6in) tall
Key features
Similar to autumn gentian but tiny, with upper leaves more widely spaced, broadly spear-shaped or oval; flowers bluish purple; sepals unequal, spreading
Flowering time
May–early November

● **Early gentian**
Gentianella anglica
Habitat and distribution
Scarce in short, dry grassland, mainly on chalk and limestone, including cliff-tops and dunes north to Lincolnshire
Size 2–13cm (¾–5in) tall, sometimes up to 20cm (8in) tall
Key features
Similar to dune gentian but upper leaves spear-shaped; flowers early, pale purple or whitish; sepals nearly equal
Flowering time
May–June

DID YOU KNOW?
The latin name *Gentiana* and English name gentian commemorate King Gentius of Illyria – modern-day Croatia – who lived about 500BC. He was credited by ancient writers as the discoverer of the medicinal properties of some gentians.

CENTAURY FACT FILE

● **Common centaury**
Centaurium erythraea
Habitat and distribution
Dry grassland, open scrub, sand dunes and shingle beaches; the most common centaury, but rare and mainly coastal in Scotland
Size 10–50cm (4–20in) tall
Key features
An erect annual or biennial, with a single stem; rosette of basal leaves, oblong or elliptical, 3 to 7-veined; stem leaves smaller and narrower, often pointed; flowers pink (sometimes white), tubular, with 5 spreading petal lobes, about 12mm (½in) long, in quite tight, irregular, flat-topped clusters
Flowering time
June–October

● **Lesser centaury**
Centaurium pulchellum
Habitat and distribution
Open, damp, sandy grassland, mostly by the sea, in England and Wales; rare in northern England, southern Scotland and Ireland
Size 2–20cm (¾–8in) tall
Key features
Similar to common centaury but a more slender, open annual lacking basal leaf rosette; stem leaves in 3–5 pairs; flowers bright reddish pink, stalked, less clustered
Flowering time
June–September

● **Slender centaury**
Centaurium tenuiflorum
Habitat and distribution
Found only in one locality – a damp, grassy undercliff on the Dorset coast
Size 10–35cm (4–14in) tall
Key features
Very like lesser centaury but grows taller, with more erect branches; stem leaves in 6–10 pairs; flowers white (sometimes pink), in denser, flatter-topped clusters
Flowering time
July–October

● **Seaside centaury**
Centaurium littorale
Habitat and distribution
Open, sandy grassland, near the sea, in western and northern Britain; also County Derry, Northern Ireland
Size 5–25cm (2–10in) tall
Key features
Similar to common centaury but shorter with several stems; basal leaves thicker, leathery, strap or spoon-shaped, 3-veined; stem leaves blunt, 1-veined; flowers slightly deeper more bluish pink, in dense, flat-topped clusters
Flowering time
June–September

● **Perennial centaury**
Centaurium scilloides
Habitat and distribution
Very rare in short seaside turf, dunes and cliff-tops in Pembrokeshire only
Size 5–30cm (2–12in) tall
Key features
A perennial with sprawling, non-flowering shoots and erect flowering stems; leaves oval or spear-shaped; relatively large flowers pink, tubular, with 5 spreading petal lobes, 15mm (⅝in) long, in small clusters
Flowering time
June–November

Seaside centaury prefers mature sand dunes and sandy places near the sea. It grows on the coasts of Wales, northern England, Scotland and County Derry in Ireland.

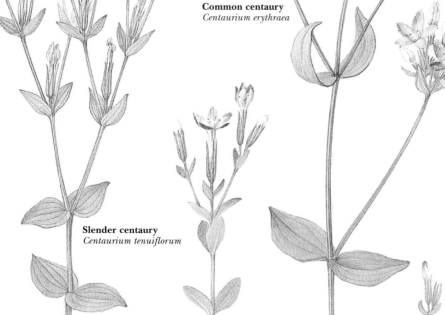

Common centaury
Centaurium erythraea

Slender centaury
Centaurium tenuiflorum

Lesser centaury
Centaurium pulchellum

Perennial centaury
Centaurium scilloides

Seaside centaury
Centaurium littorale

CENTAURY FACT FILE

● **Yellow centaury**
Cicendia filiformis
Habitat and distribution
Inconspicuous on damp, open, peaty or sandy ground, mostly near the sea, in south-west Wales, parts of southern England and south-west Ireland
Size 1–10cm (½–4in) tall, sometimes taller
Key features
A tiny, slender annual with an erect, unbranched or scarcely branched stem; leaves narrowly spear-shaped; flowers yellow, tubular, with 4 short petal lobes, about 5mm (¼in) long
Flowering time
June–October

● **Guernsey centaury**
Exaculum pusillum
Habitat and distribution
Rare and inconspicuous in damp sand dune slacks in Guernsey
Size 1–10cm (½–4in) tall
Key features
A slender, branched annual; leaves narrowly spear-shaped; flowers pink or cream, tubular, with 4 spreading petal lobes, about 5mm (¼in) long
Flowering time
July–September

● **Yellow-wort**
Blackstonia perfoliata
Habitat and distribution
Dry, lime-rich grassland and sand dunes in southern and eastern England north to Northumbria; also found on Welsh coasts and in central Ireland
Size 10–50cm (4–20in) tall
Key features
An erect, greyish green annual; basal leaves in a rosette, stem leaves in fused pairs, triangular-oval shaped; flowers yellow, with a short tube and 6–8 spreading petals, about 10mm (½in) across, held in a branched cluster
Flowering time
June–October

The eight-petalled, bright yellow flowers and waxy, grey leaves of yellow-wort are unmistakable. The plant grows on chalk grassland and dunes, but not in Scotland.

The yellow centaury is found on open, damp, sandy and peaty sites, especially on heaths close to the sea, but it is becoming scarce.

Yellow centaury
Cicendia filiformis

Guernsey centaury
Exaculum pusillum

Yellow-wort
Blackstonia perfoliata

Large clumps of autumn gentian grow on chalk grassland that at one time has been ploughed or dug over and is sparsely turfed.

WILDLIFE WATCH

Where do gentians and centauries grow?

● Gentians are plants of unimproved pasture, so they indicate species-rich habitats. Many are coastal and most grow in dry grassland over chalk and limestone, flowering in late summer and autumn.

● Many gentians are probably overlooked, either through confusion with other species or because they flower later in the year when fewer people are searching for wild flowers.

● Several scarcer gentians may have local strongholds, such as marsh gentian on damp heaths in southern England, and yellow centaury on open, peaty ground in County Cork and Kerry in Ireland. In May the Burren of County Clare is turned an intense shade of blue by the glorious flowers of spring gentian. This rare species is found at only one other site, in Upper Teesdale.

Salt-marsh plants

Oraches, sea-purslanes, seablites, glassworts and sea beet not only stabilise salt marshes but turn them into a blaze of colour. These tough little plants may also invade inland gardens and wasteground.

Members of the family Chenopodiaceae, also known as goosefoot, salt marsh plants thrive in coastal regions. The different species are not hard to distinguish. Oraches are the most complex group, made more so by frequent interbreeding and variable growth form. They can be recognised by a pair of flap-like bracts around each fruit and by the lower leaves, which often occur in opposite pairs.

Seablites have cylindrical leaves while glassworts look like miniature cacti, with fleshy, cylindrical stems and spreading branches. Sea-purslane and shrubby seablite are both woody shrubs.

The structure and appearance of the goosefoots reveal how well they are adapted for life in a harsh coastal environment. For example, the thick fleshy

▼ In sheltered estuaries where the ground is fairly stable, salt marshes develop at the edge of mud flats and distinct zones of hardy plant life can be seen.

stems and leaves help to conserve water. The tissues accumulate sodium salts and nitrogen-based chemicals, which help prevent fluids from being sucked out of the plant into the high-salt environment by the process of osmosis.

Salt tolerance

For most plants salt is a poison, but the goosefoots are adapted to deal with it. They are known as halophytes, which means 'salt-loving', although a better description would be 'salt-tolerating'. With their ability to thrive where most plants would perish, several of these plants are important to the stability of the salt marsh.

Glasswort binds the loose mud of the lower salt marsh, helping to prevent coastal erosion. Sea-purslane forms dense stands along the meandering creeks, building up the soil by trapping mud during high tides. Shrubby seablite colonises and helps to bind shingle banks. Plants that grow on the open salt

marsh, or sand or shingle beaches, pave the way for more plants and animals to move in in the future.

Edible plants

Several salt marsh plants are edible. Sea beet is related to cultivated varieties of beet and will hybridise with them. The young leaves are an alternative to spinach, as are the leaves of the various oraches. Glasswort is still collected from the wild, especially in Norfolk, and sold as samphire. This summer delicacy is a worthy substitute for asparagus.

▲ Glasswort, or marsh samphire, is an early coloniser of bare mudflats. It inhabits the lowest zone of salt marshes, turning red or pinkish in autumn.

Many of these plants are common but some are scarce. The annual sea-purslane, for example, is included in the Red Data Book of Britain's rarest plants, and is protected by the Wildlife and Countryside Act. At one time this plant was thought to be extinct but it was rediscovered in 1987 and can now be found in just one salt marsh in the entire British Isles.

DANGER!

Salt marshes and shingle beaches can be hazardous places. Be sure to check tide times to avoid being cut off at high tide.

SALT-MARSH PLANTS FACT FILE

● Sea beet
Beta vulgaris variety *maritima*
Habitat and distribution
Cliffs, rocks, sea walls, shingle
beaches and strand lines; scarce
in Scotland
Size 20–80cm (8–32in) tall
Key features
A conspicuous, hairless biennial or
perennial with sprawling or semi-erect,
leafy, red-striped stems; leaves dark
green, shiny, leathery, untoothed,
lower ones triangular; flowers
yellowish, small, in narrow, leafy
spikes; fruits in corky clusters
Flowering time
June–September

● Frosted orache
Atriplex laciniata
Habitat and distribution
Sandy seashores; often as part of
strand line
Size 10–30cm (4–12in) long
Key features
A silvery-white, sprawling or weakly
erect annual, stems buff or pinkish;
leaves diamond-shaped, irregularly
toothed, with dense powdery texture;
flowers yellowish green, minute, in
short spikes at base of upper leaves;
paired, flap-like bracts around fruits
united to halfway
Flowering time
July–September

● Grass-leaved orache
Atriplex littoralis
Habitat and distribution
Upper salt marshes and base of sea
walls in sandier areas, also occurs on
road verges inland; rare in Ireland
Size 30–150cm (1–5ft) tall
Key features
An erect, branched, leafy annual;
leaves strap-shaped, untoothed or
slightly toothed; flowers greenish,
minute, in slender, leafy spikes; paired,
flap-like bracts around fruits united at
base, toothed
Flowering time
July–September

● Spear-leaved orache
Atriplex prostrata
Habitat and distribution
Inland gardens and wasteground, and
upper parts of salt marshes
Size 10–70cm (4–28in) tall
Key features
A prostrate or erect, branched annual;
slightly powdery leaves triangular, cut
off abruptly at the base, with pair of
large basal teeth at right angles to
stalk; flowers greenish, minute, in
loose spikes; paired, flap-like bracts
around fruits united at base only,
slightly toothed
Flowering time
July–September

● Early orache
Atriplex praecox
Similar to spear-leaved orache but
purplish red from late summer and not
more than 10cm (4in) tall. A scarce
plant of sheltered sand or shingle
beaches in Scotland.

● Long-stalked orache
Atriplex longipes
Similar to spear-leaved orache but
always erect and bracts around fruit
stalked. Grows up to 80cm (32in) tall in
brackish, marsh vegetation on some
coasts of north to central Scotland

● Common orache
Atriplex patula
Habitat and distribution
Cultivated and disturbed ground,
including seashores
Size 20–100cm (8–39in) tall
Key features Similar to spear-leaved
orache but leaves more powdery; erect
or sprawling stems with branches
usually longer and more profuse;
leaves narrowing into stalk, with basal
teeth pointing forwards
Flowering time
July–September

● Babington's orache
Atriplex glabriuscula
Habitat and distribution
Shingly seashores
Size 20–40cm (8–16in) tall
Key features
Similar to spear-leaved orache but
usually prostrate, more compact
and leaves very powdery;
diamond-shaped, paired, flap-like
bracts around fruits, united to
halfway or greater, more toothed
Flowering time
July–September

● Sea-purslane
Atriplex portulacoides
Habitat and distribution
Salt marshes, especially along creeks,
north to the Solway Firth and Tweed;
eastern and southern coasts of Ireland
Size 20–100cm (8–39in) tall
Key features
A sprawling, densely branched,
greyish, evergreen shrublet; leaves
powdery grey, elliptical, untoothed,
blunt; flowers yellowish green,
minute, in short, slender spikes;
fruits unstalked
Flowering time
July–September

● Annual sea-purslane
Atriplex pedunculata
Habitat and distribution
Formerly scattered from Kent to
Lincolnshire, now at one location only
Size 10–30cm (4–12in) tall
Key features
Similar to sea-purslane, but a branched
annual with distinctly stalked fruits
Flowering time
July–September

**Silvery patches of frosted
orache are seen along sandy
coasts around Britain. The
plant usually lives along the
high-water mark.**

Frosted orache
Atriplex laciniata

Sea beet
Beta vulgaris
variety *maritima*

**The large, leathery leaves of
sea beet straggle across sea
walls, shingle and wasteground.**

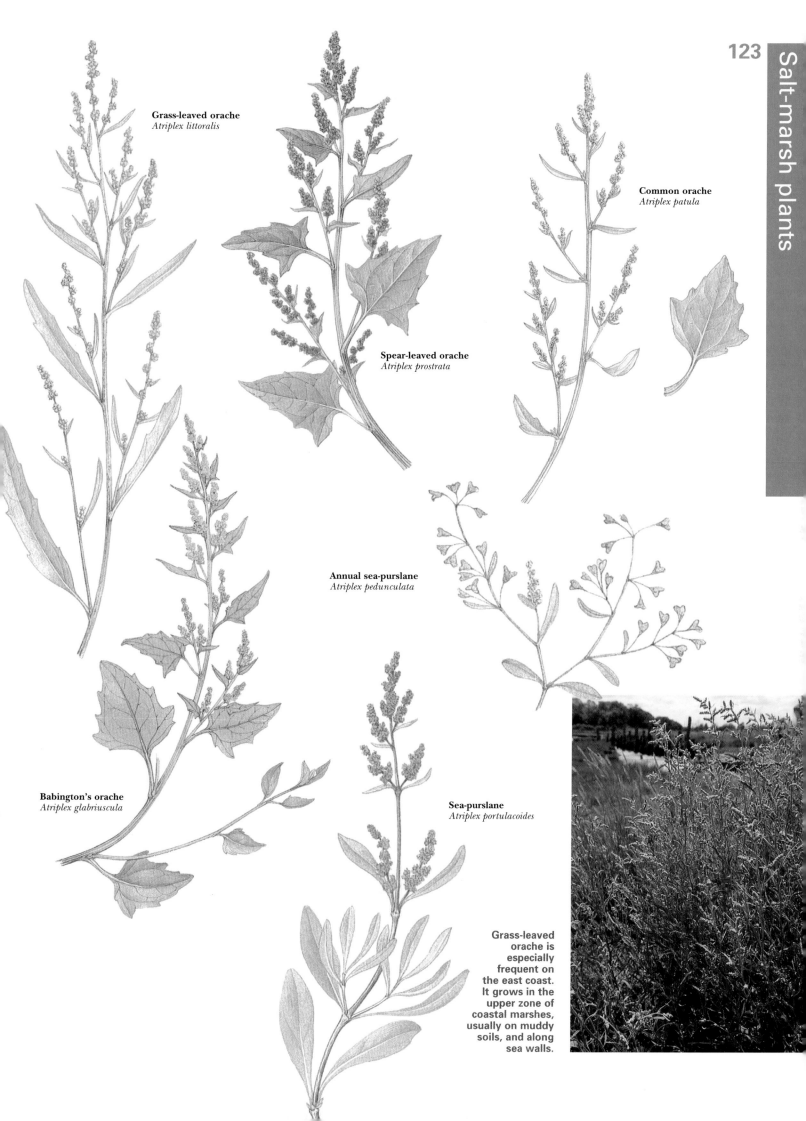

Grass-leaved orache
Atriplex littoralis

Spear-leaved orache
Atriplex prostrata

Common orache
Atriplex patula

Annual sea-purslane
Atriplex pedunculata

Babington's orache
Atriplex glabriuscula

Sea-purslane
Atriplex portulacoides

Grass-leaved orache is especially frequent on the east coast. It grows in the upper zone of coastal marshes, usually on muddy soils, and along sea walls.

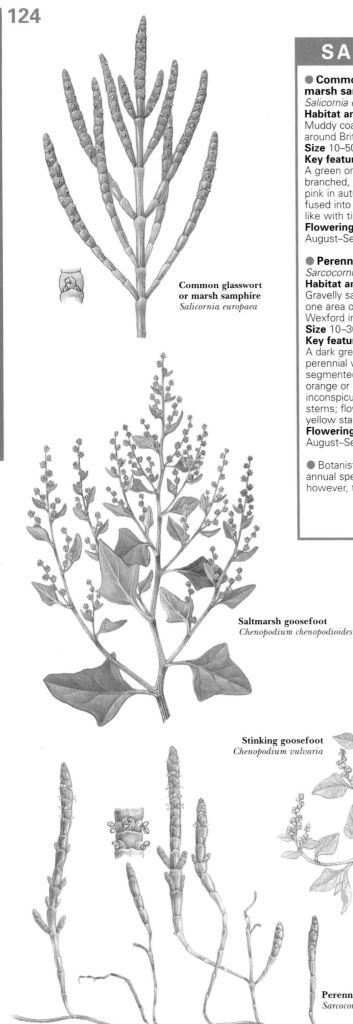

Common glasswort or marsh samphire
Salicornia europaea

Saltmarsh goosefoot
Chenopodium chenopodioides

Stinking goosefoot
Chenopodium vulvaria

Perennial glasswort
Sarcocornia perennis

SALT-MARSH PLANTS FACT FILE

● **Common glasswort or marsh samphire**
Salicornia europaea
Habitat and distribution
Muddy coastal and estuarine salt marshes around Britain and Ireland
Size 10–50cm (4–20in) tall
Key features
A green or yellowish green, erect, much branched, cactus-like annual; turns red or pink in autumn; leaves inconspicuous, fused into the fleshy stems; flowers scale-like with tiny, pale yellow stamens
Flowering time
August–September

● **Perennial glasswort**
Sarcocornia perennis
Habitat and distribution
Gravelly salt marshes in southern England, one area of north Wales and County Wexford in Ireland
Size 10–30cm (4–12in) tall
Key features
A dark green, cactus-like, tussock-forming perennial with creeping stems and erect, segmented shoots that turn yellow to orange or reddish in autumn; leaves inconspicuous, fused into the fleshy stems; flowers scale-like with tiny, pale yellow stamens; fruits tiny, inconspicuous
Flowering time
August–September

● Botanists recognise at least seven other annual species of glasswort in Britain; however, they are difficult to separate.

● **Saltmarsh goosefoot**
Chenopodium chenopodioides
Habitat and distribution
Rare on muddy shingle and beside salt-marsh ditches in a few areas of south-east England
Size 10–30cm (4–12in) tall
Key features
A sprawling or weakly erect annual; leaves powdery, triangular, untoothed or slightly toothed, a pair of large basal teeth at right angles to the stalk; flowers greenish, minute, in dense, spike-like clusters; fruits without flap-like bracts
Flowering time
July–October

● **Red goosefoot**
Chenopodium rubrum
Similar to saltmarsh goosefoot. A plant of rich soils that sometimes occurs in salt marshes, it has jagged-toothed leaves

● **Stinking goosefoot**
Chenopodium vulvaria
Habitat and distribution
Rare on shingle or bare ground, in dry salt marshes and on cliff tops in parts of south-east England
Size 10–40cm (4–16in) long
Key features
A prostrate or weakly erect, much branched annual, smelling of rotten fish when bruised; powdery leaves, more or less triangular, with a single pair of blunt basal teeth; flowers greyish green, minute, in dense, spike-like clusters; fruits without flap-like bracts
Flowering time
July–September

Perennial glasswort grows in the middle levels of the salt marsh where there is a mixture of gravel and mud.

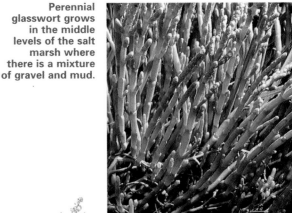

SALT-MARSH PLANTS FACT FILE

● **Annual seablite or common seablite**
Suaeda maritima
Habitat and distribution
Salt marshes and tidal mud
Size 5–30cm (2–12in) tall
Key features
A prostrate or erect, branched annual; stems reddish; leaves dark bluish green turning reddish, narrow, cylindrical, pointed; flowers green or purplish red, tiny, in clusters where leaves meet stems
Flowering time
July–October

● **Shrubby seablite**
Suaeda vera
Habitat and distribution
Coastal shingle and sand, especially where it adjoins salt marshes, from Dorset to Lincolnshire
Size 30–120cm (1–4ft) tall
Key features
An erect, branched, densely leafy, evergreen shrub; greyish leaves short, narrow, cylindrical, blunt; flowers yellowish green, minute, in clusters where leaves meet stems
Flowering time
May–September

● **Prickly saltwort**
Salsola kali
Habitat and distribution
Seen on and around the strand lines of sandy seashores; has also been introduced around ports
Size 10–50cm (4–20in) tall
Key features
An untidy, half-prostrate, branched, greyish or bluish green annual, with tough, often pink-striped stems; leaves fleshy, narrow, cylindrical, spine-tipped; flowers greenish, minute, solitary where leaves meet stems; fruits with winged margin
Flowering time
July–October

WILDLIFE WATCH

Where can I find salt-marsh plants?

● Most oraches and their relatives occur in salt marshes and on or near seashore strand lines, especially where sand or shingle is mixed with mud. Glassworts colonise open mud.

● Common and spear-leaved orache are prevalent on ploughed, dug-over or otherwise disturbed land, or on waste ground and rubbish tips, especially around coastal towns.

Prickly saltwort
Salsola kali

Shrubby seablite is a rather scarce evergreen shrub of southern and eastern England. Where it does occur, it forms dense colonies on beaches and the upper zones of salt marshes.

Annual seablite or Common seablite
Suaeda maritima

Shrubby seablite
Suaeda vera

Index

Acknowledgments

Photographs: Front cover Woodfall Wild Images, inset Mike Lane; Back cover Frank Lane Picture Agency/A R Hamblin; 1 Frank Lane Picture Agency/H Huatala; 2-3 Ardea, London/Bob Gibbons; 4 NHPA/G Bernard; 5 (t) NHPA/J Meech, (b) Nature Picture Library/J Rotman; 6 (bl) NP/Howard Clark, (bc,br) NP; 7(bl) NP/C Carver, (bc) NP/A Cleave, (br) NP/Hugh Miles; 8(bl,bc) NP/Paul Sterry, (br) NP; 9(bl) NP, (bc,br) NP/Paul Sterry; 10-11 Natural Visions; 12(t) Aquila/R Thomas, (b) FLPA/Flip de Nooyer, Photo Natura; 13(c) Ardea/Chris Knights; 14(tl) NHPA/Mike Lane, (tr) FLPA/D Tinning, (cr) FLPA/Rene Krekels, Foto Natura, (b) NHPA/Helio van Ingen; 15(tc) NP/D Osborn, (tr) FLPA/AE Hamblin; 16(tl) FLPA/R Tidman, (tr) FLPA/W Meinderts, (b) FLPA/T Hamblin; 17(tl) NP/EA Janes, (b) NP/P Sterry; 18(c) NHPA/J Meech, (br) NP/P Sterry; 19(tc) Ardea/R Richter, (tr) NPL/D Nill, (bl) NHPA/Mike Leach, (br) NPL/G Dore; 20(tc) FLPA/Ian Rose, (tr) Ardea/Bob Gibbons, (b) NHPA/J Meech; 21(cl) NPL/D Nill, (br) NV; 22(tr) NHPA, (cr) NPL/T Martin, (b) NPL/C Packham; 23(tl) FLPA/Fritz van Daalen, Foto Natura, (tr) NPL/A Tabor, (b) BC/S Nielson; 24(cl,cr) Laurie Campbell; 24-25(b) Planet Earth/R Cottle; 25(tl) NPL/A Cleave, (tr) NHPA/M Lane, (c) WW/D Element, (br) Windrush/D Tipling; 26(tl) NP/Craig Cooper, (tr) Sue Scott, (cr) NV/ Heather Angel, (bl) NP/A Cleave, (br) BC/Geoff Dore; 27(tl) OSF/C Knights, (tc) WW/Bob Gibbons, (tr) NP/R Tidman, (b) NP/R Bush; 28(cl) NHPA/L Campbell, (b) WW/N Hicks; 29(tr) Sue Scott, (cl) Ardea/D Dixon, (cr) NHPA/GI Barnard, (br) Sue Scott; 30(tlu) NV, (tl) NP/SC Bisserot, (tr) NHPA/D Heuchlin, (cl) NP/Oene Moedt, Foto Natura, (c) Ardea/D Dixon, (bl) NV; 31(tr) NV/Heather Angel, (cru,bl) David Chapman, (cr) Ardea/P Morris; 32(cr) Mike Read; 32-33 Ardea, London/Bob Gibbons, 33(tl) Ardea/M Putland, (cu) Midsummer Books, (c) Mike Read; 34(tl) Sue Scott, (tr) NP/B Burbidge, (blu) Sue Scott, (bl) Mike Read; 35(tr) David Chapman, (cl,c) Sue Scott, (b) WW/D Woodfall; 36(bl) NHPA/D Watts, 36-37(b) RSPB/Andy Hay; 37(tl) FLPA/WS Clark, (tr) Windrush/R Brooks, (cr) NP/T Wharton, (br) Windrush/D Tipling; 38(tl) BC/H Reinhard, (tr) FLPA/R Wilmhurst, (cl,br) NP/Paul Sterry, (c) Windrush/D Tipling; 39(tl) NP/Paul Sterry, (tr) Windrush/D Tipling, (cru) Ardea, (b) NP/Paul Sterry; 40(tl) FLPA/R Brooks, (tr) NP/EA Janes, (cl) NP/Paul Sterry, (cr) Windrush/D Tipling, (b) RSPB/Andy Hay; 41(cr) FLPA, (bl) RSPB/Robert Horne; 42-43 Woodfall Wild Images; 44(r) NV/ Heather Angel; 45(tr) Ardea/Ian Beames, (b) NP; 46(tl,bcu) NV/Heather Angel, (cr,bl) OSF/GA MacLean; 48(tr) BC/J Burton, (c) FLPA/M Withers, (b) NP/Paul Sterry; 49(b) BC/J Markham, (br) Sue Scott; 50(b) FLPA/M Callen; 51(tr) Aquila/M Wilkes, (b) NPL; 52(tr) FLPA/R Wilmhurst; 53(tl) BC/G McCarthy, (tc) Mike Read, (tr) FLPA/R Wilmhurst, (cl) BC, (c) NHPA/H&V van Ingen, (cru) FLPA/J van Arkel, (cr) FLPA/M Smith, (br) BC; 54(tr) Mike Read, (cl) David Chapman, (c) Windrush/H Kokkonen, (cr) Windrush/D Tipling, (bl) NHPA/H&V van Ingen; 55(tr) NPL/M Wilkes, (b) BC/P van Gallen; 56(tr) BC/G McCarthy, (bl) BC/W Laniken; 57(tc) NV/Heather Angel, (tr) FLPA/R Wilmhurst, (cl) NV/Jason Venus, (cr) FLPA/W Wisniewski; 58(tr) FLPA/R Wilmhurst, (br) FLPA/AR Hamblin; 59(tl) NP/EA Janes, (br) NP/C Knights; 60(tr) BC/G Langsbury, (clu) FLPA/M Callen, (cl) NP/TD Bonsall, (bl) NV/Heather Angel; 61(cl) NP/TD Bonsall; 62(b) FLPA/ H Huatala; 64(tl) FLPA/R Brookes, (bl) FLPA/R Wilmhurst; 65(tl) FLPA/R Wilmhurst, (cl,bl) NP/HD Brandel; 66(tl) FLPA/R Wilmhurst, (cl,bl) NP/Paul Sterry; 67 WW/M Powles; 68(tl) BC/J Burton, (tr,bl) NV/Heather Angel; 69(tr) FLPA/WS Pitt, (b) FLPA/G Marcoaldi; 70(tl) NP/SC Bisserot, (tr) FLPA/G Laci, (b) NHPA/D Heuclin; 71(cr) BC, (b) NP; 72(tr) FLPA/SC Montanari, (c) Midsummer Books, (br) NV/Heather Angel; 73(tr) Sue Scott, (bl) Planet Earth/J Johansson; 74(tl,tr) Sue Scott, (b) Frank Blackburn; 75(cr) PWW/KG Preston-Mafham, (b) NHPA/G Bernard, 76(tl) PWW/KG Preston-Mafham, (tr) OSF/J Cooke, (b) FLPA/D Grewcock; 77(t) NHPA/G Gainsburgh, (c) OSF/H Taylor; 78(tr) NHPA/GI Bernard, (bl,bc) NHPA/C Milkins, (br) BC/K Taylor; 79(l) Andrew Gagg; 80(tc,cr) Andrew Gagg; 81(tl) NV/Heather Angel, (tc) NP/Paul Sterry, (cr) NI/Bob Gibbons; 82(cl) NP/J Russell, (br) NP/B Burbidge; 83(tc,tr) Andrew Gagg, (bl) Laurie Campbell; 84(tl,cl,cr) Andrew Gagg; 85 NHPA/Bill Coster; 86(b) BC/C&S Hood; 87(tr,b) BC/G McCarthy; 88(tr) BC/A Potts, (cr) BC/G McCarthy, (bl) BC/R Jordan; 89(tr) Sealfotos Ltd, (c) NP/EA Janes, (b) BC/C&S Hood; 90(b) NHPA/Alan Williams; 91(tr) OSF/D Green, (c) NP/Paul Sterry, (br) Aquila/RT Mills; 92(bl) FLPA/R Brooks; 93(tl) WW/M Lane, (tc,cl) FLPA/M Withers, (c) FLPA/R Brooks, (br) NP/Paul Sterry; 94(b) FLPA/Flip de Nooyer, Foto Natura; 95(tr) FLPA/R Wilmhurst, (b) FLPA/AE Hamblin; 96(tl) NP/P Newman, (tr) NHPA/J Buckingham, (cl) NPL/J Cancalosi; 97(t) OSF/D Tipling; 98(tl) Windrush/C Knights, (tc) NHPA/L Campbell, (tr) Windrush/G Langsbury, (cl) Ardea/C Knights, (c) FLPA/R Brooks, (cr) NP/BR Hughes, (b) FLPA/R Wilmhurst; 99(tl) David Chapman, (tr) Planet Earth/A Geidemark, (b) FLPA/AE Hamblin; 100(b) NPL/C Packham; 101(c) OSF/M Hamblin, (br) NSc/R Revels; 102(cl) BC/C Varndell, (cr) NHPA/J Le Moigne, (bl) FLPA/M Withers, (bc) FLPA/S Johansson, (br) Laurie Campbell; 103(tl) FLPA/M Withers, (tr) NHPA/A Williams; 104(b) NPL/J Rotman; 105(tr) Midsummer Books, (br) Planet Earth/K Lucas; 106(tl) unknown, (tc) Midsummer Books, (br) Planet Earth/G Douwma; 107(tr) NHPA/T McDonald, (bl) Planet Earth; 108(tr) BC/A Purcell, (b) NHPA/R Waller; 109(tl) NV/Heather Angel, (tr) OSF/LM Crowhurst, (bl) BC/K Taylor, (br) Ardea/P Morris; 110(l,br) NV/Heather Angel; 111(tl) NHPA/R Waller, (tc) NP/N Callow, (tr) OSF/R Jackman, (cr) FLPA/D Wilson, (bl) NV/Heather Angel; 112-113 unknown; 114(cr) OSF/RL Manuel, (b) NPL/N Benvie; 115(tl,tr) OSF/London Scientific Films, (cr) Planet Earth/R Arnold, (br) NHPA/A Bannister; 116(bl) NHPA/J Gifford, (br) NHPA/R Tompson; 117(cr) OSF/D Fox, (bl) FLPA/T Wharton; 119(tr) NHPA/D Woodfall; 120 Andrew Gagg; 121(tr) OSF/M Chillmaid, (b) FLPA/R Tidman; 122(tr,bc) NP; 123-125 Andrew Gagg.

Illustrations: 46-48, 52-54, 56-58, 60-61, 92-93, 96-97, 102-103 John Ridyard; 63(t), 64(r), 65(r), 66(r) Robert Morton; 80-84, 117-120, 122-125 Ian Garrard; 105 Keith Linsell.

Key to Photo Library Abbreviations: BC = Bruce Coleman Ltd, FLPA = Frank Lane Photo Agency, NHPA = Natural History Photo Agency, NI= Natural Image, NP = Nature Photographers, NPL = Nature Picture Library, NSc = Natural Science Photos, NV = Heather Angel/Natural Visions, OSF = Oxford Scientific Films, PW = Premaphotos Wildlife, WW = WW Wild.

Key to position abbreviations: b = bottom, bl = bottom left, blu = bottom left upper, br = bottom right, bru = bottom right upper, c = centre, cl = centre left, clu = centre left upper, cr = centre right, cru = centre right upper, cu = centre upper, l = left, r = right, sp = spread, t = top, tl = top left, tlu = top left upper, tr = top right, tru = top right upper.

Wildlife Watch
Waterside & Coast in Autumn

Published by the Reader's Digest Association Limited, 2005

The Reader's Digest Association Limited
11 Westferry Circus, Canary Wharf
London E14 4HE

We are committed to both the quality of our products and the service we provide to our customers, so please feel free to contact us on 08705 113366, or via our website at: www.readersdigest.co.uk

If you have any comments about the content of our books you can contact us at: gbeditorial@readersdigest.co.uk

® Reader's Digest, The Digest and the Pegasus logo are registered trademarks of The Reader's Digest Association, Inc., of Pleasantville, New York, USA

Reader's Digest General Books:
Editorial Director Cortina Butler
Art Director Nick Clark
Series Editor Christine Noble
Project Art Editor Julie Bennett
Prepress Accounts Manager Penelope Grose

This book was designed, edited and produced by Eaglemoss Publications Ltd, based on material first published as the partwork *Wildlife of Britain*

For Eaglemoss:
Editors Celia Coyne, Marion Paull, Helen Spence, John Woodward
Art Editor Phil Gibbs
Consultant Jonathan Elphick
Publishing Manager Nina Hathway

Copyright © Eaglemoss Publications Ltd/Midsummer Books Ltd 2005

Printed and bound in Europe by Arvato Iberia

CONCEPT CODE: UK 0133/G/S
BOOK CODE: 630-006-01
ISBN: 0 276 44054 4
ORACLE CODE: 356200013H.00.24